Fabulous Paper Airplanes

E. Richard Churchill

Illustrated by James Michaels

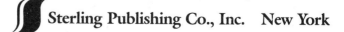
Sterling Publishing Co., Inc.   New York

For Chum, who loves airplanes, airports, and everything about flying.

With special thanks to Jason and my wife's students at Brentwood Middle School in Greeley, Colorado, for their designs, suggestions, and interest in the airplanes in this book, and to the paper airplane fliers in London's parks who so willingly shared their ideas and designs with me.

Edited by Keith L. Schiffman

Library of Congress Cataloging-in-Publication Data

Churchill, E. Richard (Elmer Richard)
    Fabulous paper airplanes / by E. Richard Churchill ; illustrated
by James Michaels.
         p.   cm.
    Includes index.
    Summary: Explains the basic principles of flight and gives folding
instructions for twenty-nine paper airplanes.
    ISBN 0-8069-8342-6
    1. Paper airplanes—Juvenile literature. [1. Paper airplanes.
2. Handicraft.] I. Michaels, James ill. II. Title.
TL778.C48 1991
745.592—dc20   91-10490
                                                      CIP
                                                           AC

10 9 8 7 6 5 4 3 2 1

First paperback edition published in 1992 by
Sterling Publishing Company, Inc.
387 Park Avenue South, New York, N.Y. 10016
© 1991 by E. Richard Churchill
Distributed in Canada by Sterling Publishing
% Canadian Manda Group, P.O. Box 920, Station U
Toronto, Ontario, Canada M8Z 5P9
Distributed in Great Britain and Europe by Cassell PLC
Villiers House, 41/47 Strand, London WC2N 5JE, England
Distributed in Australia by Capricorn Link Ltd.
P.O. Box 665, Lane Cove, NSW 2066
Manufactured in the United States of America
All rights reserved

Sterling ISBN 0-8069-8342-6 Trade
               0-8069-8343-4 Paper

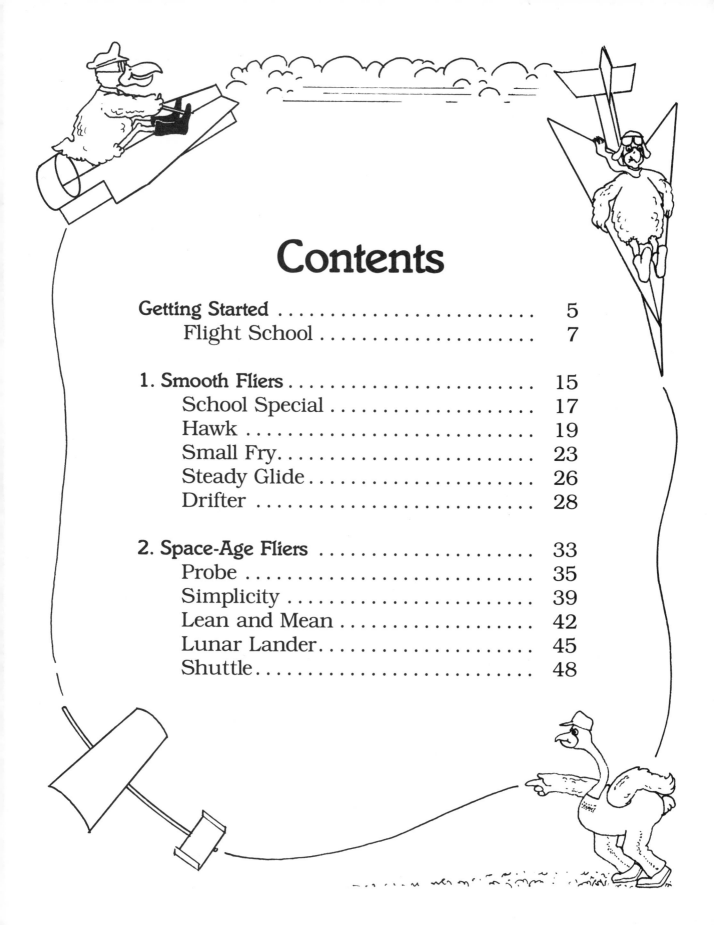

Contents

Getting Started

Making and flying paper airplanes is fabulous fun. A sheet of paper, a few folds, and a minute or two are all you need to get started. From then on, the sky's the limit as you build and fly the paper airplanes described in this book. Soon you'll move on to designs and changes of your own.

A sheet of notebook paper will get you started. Just in case you're someone who likes to plan ahead, here's a list of supplies you'll be using as you build these airplanes. You won't use every item on each airplane, however.

1. Paper: Notebook paper makes great airplanes. Typing paper or computer pages will also work perfectly.

2. Scissors: Sometimes you'll need to make cuts.

3. Paper clips: You'll use these to get your paper airplanes in proper balance for great flights.

4. Tape: Cellophane tape is easy to use. Small strips of masking tape will work just as well (most of the time).

5. Glue or staples: Sometimes you'll want to use glue or staples instead of tape.

6. Ruler: Sometimes you'll need to do a bit of measuring.

7. Pencil: Dots and lines help with some of the airplanes.

8. File cards or old file folders: For special occasions.

9. Cereal box(es): Occasionally you'll need a piece of this lightweight cardboard.

10. Drinking straws: You'll need these for some of the planes described towards the end of this book.

Some of the paper airplanes you'll be folding begin with a square piece of paper. Take a few seconds to learn to turn a rectangular sheet of notebook paper or typing paper into a square piece of paper.

Begin by folding one corner of the paper over so it looks like Illus. 1. Cut away the shaded part seen in Illus. 2. When you unfold the paper you'll have a perfectly square sheet.

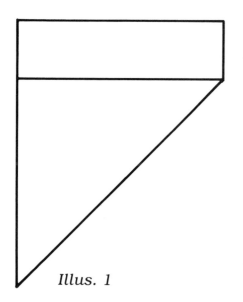

Illus. 1

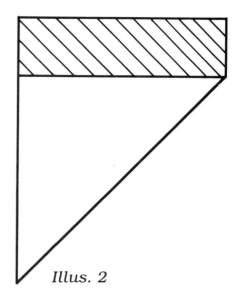

Illus. 2

Welcome aboard, crew! Your first mission is to make a square!

FLIGHT SCHOOL

Pilots spend many hours in flight school before they're qualified to fly an airplane. In flight school future pilots learn the basics of aviation—how an airplane flies and what they need to do in order to fly an airplane safely and well.

Even after earning a license and flying airplanes across the nation or even around the world, pilots still return to school for refresher courses from time to time.

This chapter is the reader's pilot's flight school. You'll learn why fabulous *paper* airplanes fly and how to make them fly better. Let's begin by learning *how* an airplane flies, and how various parts of the aircraft help it to fly. Then we'll move on to turning the folded paper airplanes into great flying machines.

Read enough of this chapter to understand exactly how airplanes fly. Then fold and fly several of the airplanes in the book. Then come back to "flight school" and read a bit more. Read how the different parts of airplanes affect the plane's flight. Begin to use the technical terms when you discuss your paper airplanes. Put to use what you learn in flight school as you fold and fly more paper airplanes.

Finish flight school by reading about what you can do to correct or change the way your paper airplanes fly. Put this knowledge to work as you keep on folding and flying new and different paper airplanes.

Don't worry if you can't remember all the terms at first. "Flight school" will always be here for you—you can turn back to it from time to time.

How Airplanes Fly Four forces influence the way airplanes fly. The drawing shown in Illus. 3 names these four forces. The arrows shown in the drawing show how each force acts upon an airplane. These four forces work on *every* airplane in the world, from commercial airlines to paper airplanes.

An airplane must have *power* to move forward. *Thrust* is the term pilots use when talking about power. Jets provide thrust for huge airliners. The force of your hand and your arm gives a paper airplane its needed thrust.

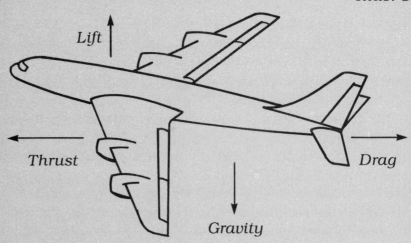

Lift · Thrust · Drag · Gravity

Lift is the second force which helps keep the airplane flying. An airplane's wings provide lift. As air moves across the curved surface on top of an airplane's wing, it creates an area of low pressure. This low air pressure provides lift. The air pressure *beneath* the wing is normal because the underside of the wing is not curved like the top of the wing.

Every airplane (whether powered by jets or by the force of your arm) has to overcome *drag* in order to fly. The pressure of the air through which the airplane flies creates drag. Drag slows down flight. The more of the plane's surface there is exposed to air, the greater the drag becomes. When an airplane's nose comes up it exposes more of the craft's surface to the air, increasing drag. If there is too much drag for the thrust and lift to overcome, the plane stalls, and it may even crash.

The fourth force acting on airplanes is *gravity*. Gravity's pull affects all things, including airplanes in flight. An aircraft has to overcome gravity's pull by combining lift and thrust in order just to get off the ground. Then gravity must *still* be overcome in order for the airplane to actually fly.

Thrust and lift combined have to be greater than the total forces of drag and gravity in order for an airplane to fly.

Now let's *really* get into "flight school" and learn how pilots talk and what the terms mean.

The first term all pilots need to know is *fuselage*. The fuselage is the body of the aircraft. It is that part of the airplane to which the wings and tail section are attached.

Now let's move on to the *control surfaces*. Any movable part of an airplane's wings or its tail assembly is a control surface. Any time you change or adjust any control surface, there will be a difference in the way the airplane flies.

Illus. 4 will serve as your introduction to our discussion of an airplane's wings.

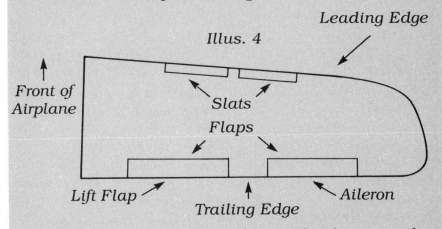

Illus. 4

Leading Edge

Front of Airplane

Slats

Flaps

Lift Flap

Aileron

Trailing Edge

To begin with, the front of an airplane's wing is the *leading edge*. (This is easy to remember—the leading edge *leads* the wing through the air.) The wing's *trailing edge* follows or *trails* the wing. The trailing edge is the *rear* edge of the wing.

Any movable control surface on the wing's trailing edge may be called a *flap*. Flaps may be pointed down to increase the curve in the airplane's wing and thereby increase the lift. You increase lift on your paper airplane by folding or bending or rolling the trailing edge of the wing down slightly.

Pilots call some of the flaps *ailerons*. Aviation engineers and pilots know that air moves faster over a curved surface than over a flat surface. The faster the air moves, the greater the lift the air supplies. During take off and when climbing during flight, pilots adjust the ailerons to give more lift. The ailerons are extended out from the wing and pushed downwards at an angle. This gives the wing more of a curved shape and it also provides extra lift.

Some of the larger airplanes have *lift flaps* along the wing's trailing edge. These lift flaps are closer to the fuselage than the ailerons. The purpose of the lift flap is to give even more lift during takeoff. When climbing, pilots tip the lift flaps downwards to give extra lift.

Special control surfaces on the leading edge of the wings of large airplanes are known as *slats*. These slats may be adjusted during takeoff to provide the wing with even more lift.

Illus. 5

Illus. 5 shows an airplane head-on. The tips of the wings are higher than the spot where the wings join the fuselage. This upward angle is called *dihedral*. The amount of dihedral affects both lift and the way the airplane flies.

Some airplanes have drooping wings—the wing tips are lower than the spot where the wing joins the fuselage. Airplanes with this type of wing are said to have *negative dihedral*.

If you really want to let people know that you're a "flying school" graduate, mention a wing's *camber*. Camber refers to the curve *on top* of the wing which increases the speed of air flow *over* the wing.

Let's now move back to the tail assembly. Illus. 6 shows you the basic tail portion of an airplane. Let's talk about the part of the tail extending outward from both sides of the fuselage (like little wings). This part is called the *horizontal stabilizer*. It's *horizontal* because it sticks out to the sides. It's a *stabilizer* because it helps keep the airplane stable or steady during flight.

The front of the horizontal stabilizer is its leading edge; the rear of the stabilizer is the trailing edge.

The control flap at the trailing edge of the horizontal stabilizer is known as the *elevator*. When it moves

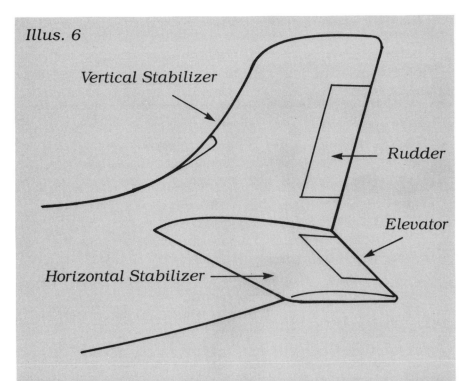

Illus. 6

Vertical Stabilizer

Rudder

Elevator

Horizontal Stabilizer

up or down it causes the airplane to gain or lose elevation.

The part of the tail section sticking straight up from the fuselage is the *vertical stabilizer*. It stands up *vertically* and it also helps to keep the airplane's flight *stable*.

The control flap at the trailing edge of the vertical stabilizer is called the *rudder*. The pilot moves the rudder to assist in turning the airplane during flight.

You don't *have* to remember all of these terms in order to fold and fly a paper airplane, but why not use the names pilots and aviation experts use? It helps to be exact when discussing aviation, and it's pretty impressive as well.

Flying Your Fabulous Paper Airplanes Now that you can talk about parts of your airplane like a commercial pilot, it's time to learn the vocabulary of flight itself.

Before we start, let's take a few seconds to discuss safety. Pilots are aware of the need for constant attention to safety while flying. You should be aware of safety, as well, especially when flying your fabulous paper airplanes outdoors.

11

Here's a *safety tip*. When you take your paper airplanes outside, some will end up on housetops or in trees. When this happens, don't try to rescue your paper airplane. Wait for the wind to bring your plane down. Meanwhile, just go inside and fold a new one—it will take only a minute or two.

Never chase a paper airplane into the street. If your plane lands in the street, check for cars before even *thinking* about going for the airplane. If a car runs over your airplane, don't worry about it—just fold a new one.

With safety in mind, let's begin to speak like aviators as we fly our paper airplanes.

All flights begin with a launch. Launching puts your airplane into the air. A quick flick of the wrist gets some airplanes flying. Others prefer a gentle movement of your entire hand. When you launch airplanes outside, you'll often find that they need a little more force to launch them than if you launch them indoors.

One of the first words you'll need to know is "*stall.*" When an airplane hesitates, or almost stops in midair it has gone into a stall. The stalled plane will then flutter to the ground. Pilots have warning lights to let them know when a stall is coming—they can then prevent it.

If your airplane stalls, you probably need to adjust its *trim*. Trim means balancing an airplane so that it flies properly. Slip a paper clip or two onto the fuselage near the nose to correct most stalls. You'll find that moving one or more clips nearer to the nose or towards the tail is often all you have to do to correct the trim and to have a smooth flight.

The opposite of a stall is a dive. A plane goes into a dive when there is too much weight near the front. Moving any paper clips towards the tail is an easy way to overcome a dive.

You can also prevent stalls and dives by bending or rolling the control surfaces on the trailing edges of the wings either up or down. Don't be afraid to experiment. Feel free to change control surfaces; learn what flight differences result from the various changes you make.

When you experiment with changes affecting your airplane's trim, try giving the wings on some airplanes more or less dihedral. This often changes their trim enough to affect the way they fly.

Some other quick trimming tips can change the flight characteristics of your fabulous paper airplanes. Try bending down the elevators on the trailing edges of the horizontal stabilizer if your airplane stalls. This tip, along with a paper clip on the nose usually can cure stalling. If you make an airplane with the stabilizer and the wing in one piece, bend a small section of the wing's trailing edge. You can always make a pair of cuts in the trailing edge to create a small control flap. This technique works for wings or for a horizontal stabilizer.

You must do just the *opposite* to prevent dives. Lighten the nose or bend control surfaces *up* on the horizontal stabilizer to correct diving.

Paper airplanes often *bank* in flight, meaning that they turn either to the right or to the left. If your airplane banks, and you prefer a straight flight, here's what to do. Bend the aileron or the trailing edge of the wing downwards on the side to which the plane is banking. You can also bend *up* the opposite aileron or trailing edge. Or, you can do both. If your plane banks to the right, bend down the right aileron or bend up the left one.

You can also bend the trailing edge of the rudder in the opposite direction of the bank. A plane banking to the right can be corrected by bending the rudder or the trailing edge of the vertical stabilizer to the left.

Try these trimming tips and see what each one does to the airplane's flight characteristics. Don't be afraid to experiment.

Learn how trim changes affect flight characteristics. Work for smooth and level flights with some airplanes. Other airplanes are better suited for fast, straight flights. Some airplanes do better with slow, looping flights.

Pilots talk about *pitch* or *degree of pitch* when the airplane's nose goes up or down. Extreme pitch often causes stalling or diving. Paper clips on the fuselage cure pitch quickly.

When one wing tips to one side or to the other during flight, your airplane is *rolling*. First make certain that both wings have the same dihedral. Make sure that the trailing edges of both wings have the same amount of bending or folding; both should provide equal lift. You could *deliberately* cause your paper airplane to roll by setting the flaps or bending the trailing edges at different angles.

If your airplane's nose turns to the right or to the left, it is *yawing*. Yawing is often caused when the vertical stabilizer is not straight up and down. Check the vertical stabilizer first if your plane develops a yaw.

You may want to give a vertical stabilizer to an airplane which yaws. Just cut out a vertical stabilizer from a file card or very light cardboard and glue or tape the stabilizer into place. Be sure the stabilizer points straight up and down.

You can make your airplane perform a 360° roll in flight. Just adjust the control surfaces until the plane spins completely around on its axis without crashing.

Inside loops are great fun. A loop is a 360° loop or circle—the plane then goes on flying. To fly an inside loop, adjust the control surfaces so that the nose comes up and keeps on coming up, forcing the airplane to finish the loop.

The *outside loop*—the airplane's nose goes down and the plane performs a complete loop or circle. Outside loops are harder to accomplish than inside loops, and are extremely dangerous to the pilots who attempt them.

Once you've mastered trimming, it's time to think about having some competition with other paper-airplane fliers. One of the most popular competition categories is *total distance covered in a single flight*. Be fair when flying outdoors—the wind must be the same for all flights.

Acrobatic-flying contests include loops, spins, banks, and rolls. Go for the most loops, the greatest banking, or the biggest number of direction changes during a single flight.

Congratulations! You have just graduated from flight school. Go out and have a *fabulous* flight!

1.
Smooth Fliers

Smooth Fliers

These paper airplanes will give you a long, smooth flight.

School Special

This smooth-flying model is called the *School Special* because it's the perfect paper airplane to make and fly while on the school playground.

Begin by folding a sheet of notebook or typing paper in half the long way. Unfold it so it lies flat in front of you.

Next, fold a corner over so your paper looks like Illus. 7. You can see from the drawing that you're using the middle fold you just made as a guide for folding corner "A."

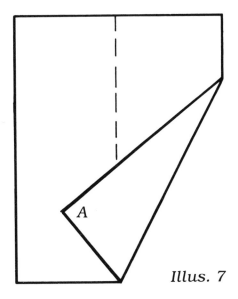

Illus. 7

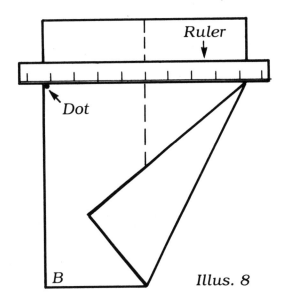

Illus. 8

Now place your ruler as shown in Illus. 8. Make a small dot (as shown in the drawing) on the side of the paper above corner "B."

Use this dot as the top limit of your second fold. This fold brings corner "B" over, so that your *School Special* looks like the one shown in Illus. 9.

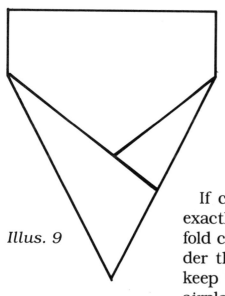

Illus. 9

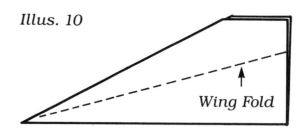

Illus. 10

Wing Fold

If corner "B" sticks out a bit instead of ending up exactly even with the first fold, that's just fine. Simply fold corner "B" over so that the extra paper is now under the airplane. Use just a bit of cellophane tape to keep this flap of paper tight against the body of the airplane.

Now fold the paper airplane down the middle. Now it looks like the one shown in Illus. 10. The dotted line shown in Illus. 10 shows where you'll make your first wing fold.

Fold down the wing closest to you and then crease the fold. You don't want the wing to come all the way down to the bottom of the plane's body or fuselage. Make the fold high enough so there is a little space between the wing's edge and the bottom of the fuselage.

Turn the airplane over and fold down the second wing. Your *School Special* should look like the one shown in Illus. 11.

Unfold the wings so your airplane looks like Illus. 12. The dotted line shows the second wing fold. When you make this fold, the lower edge of the wing will come down below the bottom of the fuselage.

Illus. 11

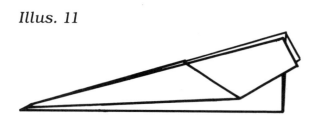

Illus. 12

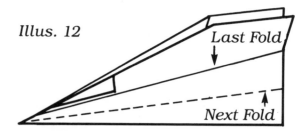

Last Fold

Next Fold

Your *School Special* is ready to fly. When you squeeze the sides of the fuselage together to launch the airplane, the top sections of both wings should form a nearly level surface. The outer portions of the wings will dip down.

Test-fly your airplane. It should go into a long, smooth glide. If it seems to stall, or hesitate in the air, try adding a paper clip to the nose.

Use the *School Special* for design testing on later models. Experiment by making different wing folds from those on this first model. Try making the upper part of the wings a bit wider or a little narrower and see how these design differences change the way the *School Special* performs.

Hawk

Hawk will give you a long, even flight. It takes just a few minutes of folding and cutting. The finished airplane is a fabulous flier.

Begin by folding a sheet of notebook paper or typing paper in half, lengthwise. Turn the paper so the fold is up and towards you, as shown in Illus. 13. Measure two inches in from the left on the upper side and mark that point with a small dot as shown in the same drawing. The dotted line shows your next fold.

Fold the right-hand corner down, so your *Hawk* looks like Illus. 14. Now turn the airplane over and fold the other side so it matches the folds you just made.

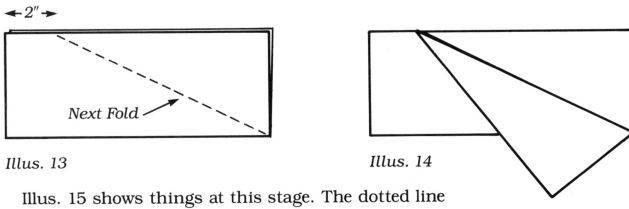

← 2″ →

Next Fold

Illus. 13

Illus. 14

Illus. 15 shows things at this stage. The dotted line indicates your next fold.

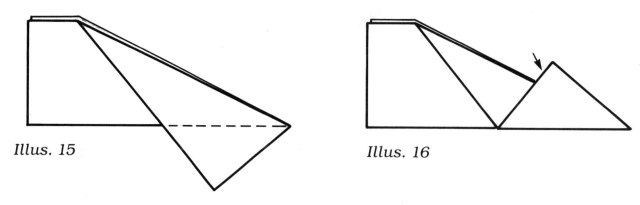

Illus. 15

Illus. 16

Fold this section of *Hawk* up along the dotted line shown in the drawing. Turn the airplane over and fold the other side up in the same manner. You've now reached the stage shown in Illus. 16.

After making the last folds, there is some extra material extending past the airplane. The arrow in Illus. 16 shows this paper. Open the airplane and fold this back over the rest of the airplane. Use a bit of cellophane tape to hold each of these flaps in place. Illus. 17 gives you a look at the construction at this stage.

Refold the *Hawk* down its middle fold. Check the lines drawn as shown in Illus. 18. Cut along these lines while the paper is folded. Be sure you hold the two halves of the paper firmly together so that the *Hawk* is exactly the same on both sides.

You'll be cutting at angles, except for the even cut along the top of the fuselage. These angles give the finished *Hawk* its special shape. Use a pencil and ruler to draw the cut lines before you use your scissors.

Illus. 17

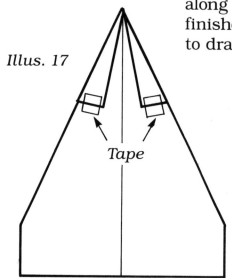

Tape

Cuts

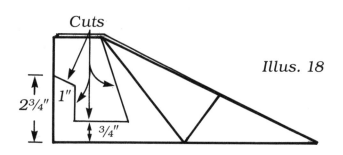

Illus. 18

$2\frac{3}{4}''$ $1''$ $\frac{3}{4}''$

20

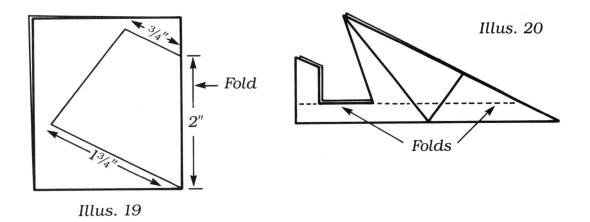

Illus. 20

Illus. 19

Now finish the tail section. Fold a small piece of paper in half and draw the vertical portion of the tail so it looks like the drawing shown in Illus. 19. Make sure the fold is on the side to which the arrow points in the drawing. The dimensions in the drawing give you a vertical stabilizer of the proper size.

The tail section of the *Hawk*, or any airplane, is made up of a vertical stabilizer and a horizontal stabilizer. You're making the vertical stabilizer now. The horizontal stabilizer is attached to the fuselage. You cut this piece just a minute ago. It can be seen very well in Illus. 20.

It's time to finish *Hawk*. Fold both the wings and the horizontal stabilizer down along the dotted lines shown in Illus. 20. Now for the final touches. Use a bit of cellophane tape to hold *Hawk's* nose together. Illus. 21 shows this step.

At the same time, slip the vertical stabilizer into place (in the fold) with the folded side facing forward. Notice that the rear of the vertical stabilizer extends about one-eighth inch behind the fuselage. The strip of tape you use to hold the rear of the fuselage together will also hold the stabilizer in place.

Illus. 21

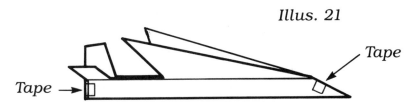

Tape the airplane's nose, not mine!

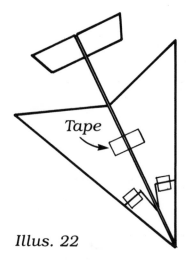

Tape

Illus. 22

Pull the wings together with a strip of tape, as shown in Illus. 22. Give *Hawk's* wings some dihedral. Dihedral (an aviation term) means that the tips of the airplane's wings are higher than the level of the wings at the fuselage.

Place one end of the cellophane tape on the right-hand wing and press it firmly into place at the point shown in Illus. 22. Don't let the other end of the tape touch the paper yet.

Lift the tips of *Hawk's* wings so that they are one inch higher than the point where the wings join the fuselage. This will give *Hawk* some dihedral. Press the loose end of the tape onto the left-hand wing. When you let go of the wing tips, they'll remain in a raised position. The tape will hold the wing tips up and give *Hawk* its dihedral.

Give *Hawk* a quick test flight. Launch it with a smooth forward motion of your hand and arm. *Hawk* may give you a long, even glide the first time you launch it. Or it may go into a dive before finishing its full glide. If that happens, check Illus. 23.

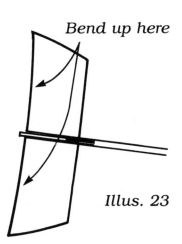

Bend up here

Illus. 23

Use your thumb and forefinger to bend up the rear edges of the horizontal stabilizer slightly. The rear of an airplane's wing or stabilizer is called the *trailing edge*. You don't want to make a fold on the horizontal stabilizer's trailing edge. Instead, try to bend up the stabilizer by rolling your thumb over the top of the material. At the same time, push up from the underside with your fingers. Just work the trailing edge upwards in a nice, smooth, bend or roll.

Now test *Hawk* again. If it stalls, your stabilizer is probably bent or rolled up a bit too much. Just smooth out some of the roll you put in place a second ago. Or, you could slip a paper clip onto *Hawk's* nose to correct the stall.

Once you get *Hawk* set up properly, it is one of the smoothest flying paper airplanes you can imagine.

Small Fry

Small Fry does a great job. It will always give you smooth flights.

Begin with a square sheet of paper. Check back to pages 5 and 6 if you don't remember how to turn a rectangular sheet of notebook paper or typing paper into a square.

Fold corner "A" over to the opposite corner and crease the fold. Then unfold the paper. Do the same for corner

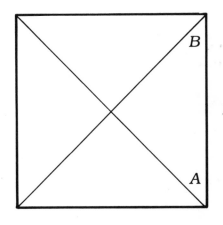

Illus. 24

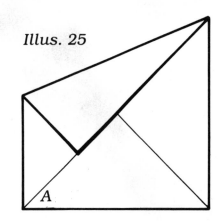

Illus. 25

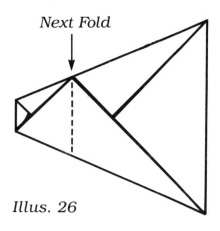

Next Fold

Illus. 26

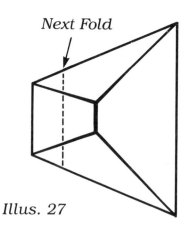

Next Fold

Illus. 27

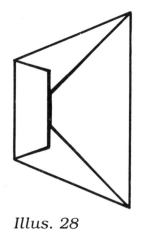

Illus. 28

"B." Your paper now has two diagonal creases, as shown, in Illus. 24. Use these creases as guidelines so you can fold *Small Fry* correctly.

Unfold the sheet and turn the paper over. The creases you just made look like ridges seen from this side. Corners "A" and "B" are now on the left side of the sheet.

Fold corner "B" down to the crease so that your paper looks like Illus. 25. Now fold corner "A" up, so that its edge just touches the crease as shown in Illus. 26. The dotted line shown in Illus. 26 shows where to make the next fold.

After making that fold, you've reached the step shown in Illus. 27. The dotted line in this drawing shows your next fold. Once this fold is made, *Small Fry* looks like the drawing in Illus. 28. Fold *Small Fry* in half down the middle so it looks like the drawing shown in Illus. 29.

The dotted line in Illus. 29 shows where to fold *Small Fry's* wings.

Illus. 29

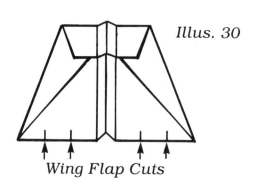

Wing Fold

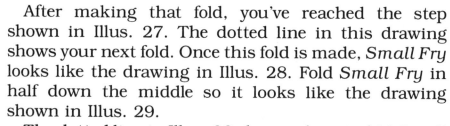

Illus. 30

Wing Flap Cuts

Fold down the wing nearer to you along the dotted line shown in the drawing. Turn the airplane over and fold the other wing into place.

When you spread the wings, your paper airplane is just about ready for its first test flight.

First, cut two little flaps into the rear of the wings. Illus. 30 shows where to make these flap cuts in the trailing edge of the wing. Make each of the four cuts only about one-quarter inch deep. Leave about one and one-half inches between each cut on each wing.

Because *Small Fry's* length from nose to tail is pretty short, these flaps will make a difference in the way the

How many more folds does this airplane need?

airplane flies. If the flaps are too deep, *Small Fry* will have difficulty flying.

These flaps will give you the same sort of effect as the effect you got from bending the horizontal stabilizers on *Hawk*. Since flaps help control the way an airplane flies, we sometimes call them control surfaces.

You may find that *Small Fry* wants to stall when you test it. If this happens, slip a paper clip onto its nose and test it again. Start with the airplane's wings extending straight out. You can give the wings a bit of upward slant or dihedral later.

Adjust the flaps by bending them upwards and experiment to see how the flaps change the way *Small Fry* performs. You'll find, for example, that when you add a paper clip to *Small Fry's* nose you'll probably need to bend the flaps upwards a bit. This will also help if you find that the nose is too heavy.

Once you have *Small Fry* balanced, or trimmed, correctly, it will go into a nice long glide for you.

Steady Glide

Begin by folding a sheet of notebook paper or typing paper in half the short way as shown in Illus. 31. Unfold the paper. Fold the bottom of the paper up, so that the bottom edge touches the middle fold. Crease this second fold. Your paper looks like Illus. 32. The dotted line in the drawing indicates your next fold.

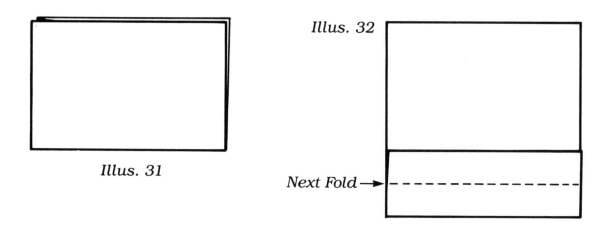

Illus. 31

Illus. 32

Next Fold →

Illus. 33 shows the state of affairs after making your next fold. The dotted line shows you your next fold.

Make the fold as indicated in Illus. 33, and then turn and fold the airplane in half so it looks like Illus. 34. Crease this fold. Think of the thick bunch of folded paper as the airplane's nose.

The dotted line in the drawing shows where you'll make the next fold. Check Illus. 34 carefully before you start folding. This fold starts and ends one-half inch from the corners of the paper.

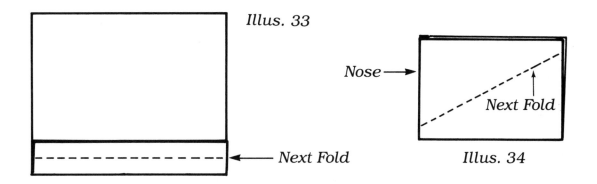

Illus. 33

Nose ⟶

Next Fold

⟵ Next Fold

Illus. 34

Fold down the wing nearer you, towards you along the dotted fold line. *Steady Glide* should now look like the drawing shown in Illus. 35.

Turn the airplane over and fold down the second wing exactly as you did with the first wing you folded. Illus. 36 shows where you are at this point.

The dotted line in Illus. 36 shows the next fold you'll make. Check the dotted line before you start work. This fold runs uphill towards the airplane's nose.

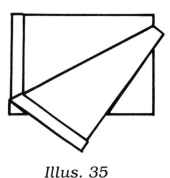

Illus. 35

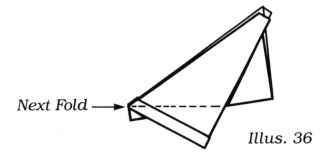

Next Fold ⟶

Illus. 36

Fold up the wing nearer to you along the dotted line. Turn the airplane over and fold the second wing exactly as you did the first. Illus. 37 shows *Steady Glide* now.

Use a small strip of cellophane tape to hold this last fold tightly in place. Illus. 37 shows the best place to tape. After taping one wing, do the same on the other wing.

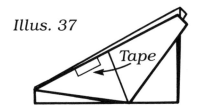

Illus. 37

Tape

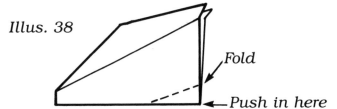

Illus. 38

Fold

⟵ Push in here

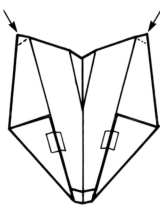

Illus. 39

Once both wings are taped into place, lift them both up and out of the way so that your *Steady Glide* looks like the drawing in Illus. 38.

Fold the fuselage towards you, along the dotted line shown in Illus. 38. Fold the fuselage back away from you, along the fold you just made. Double-folding will make your next step easier.

Hold the airplane in one hand and hold the fuselage with the other hand at the point shown by the arrow in Illus. 38. Push up on the end of the fuselage and turn the folded part inside out. When you're finished, the folded area will stick up inside the fuselage where it will act as a vertical stabilizer.

Illus. 39 shows a top view of *Steady Glide* ready for its first flight test.

Launch *Steady Glide* with a steady, forward movement of your hand and arm. More than likely, *Steady Glide* will stall. When this happens, add a paper clip to its nose (for trim) and then test it again.

Depending upon the weight of the paper you used, you may find that *Steady Glide* does its best long, smooth gliding when you add two paper clips to its nose for proper trim.

Once *Steady Glide* flies nicely, it's time to experiment with the effect of control surfaces. The two arrows shown in Illus. 39 point to the very rear tips of *Steady Glide's* wings. Bend up these two tips along the dotted lines and see how just this little change affects the airplane's flight. Next, bend the two wing tips down and see how this alters its flying characteristics. Finally, bend one tip up and the other down and launch the airplane.

By experimenting with these two little control surfaces you'll change *Steady Glide* from a long distance glider into an airplane which will dip, turn, and even fly a loop for you.

Drifter

This two-piece paper airplane will give you lots of great flying time. Begin by making *Drifter's* tail section. Cut a strip of paper about two and one-quarter inches wide and eleven inches long.

Fold the strip down the middle the long way. After creasing the fold, flatten out the strip of paper so it looks like the one shown in Illus. 40. Now fold over the two bottom corners as shown in Illus. 41. Set this strip of paper to one side for the time being.

Now you'll need a full sheet of notebook paper or typing paper to use for *Drifter's* body.

Begin by folding over one corner, as shown in Illus. 42. Fold the other corner over so the paper looks like the drawing shown in Illus. 43. Unfold the paper and turn it over.

Fold up the bottom edge so that the folded edge comes to the point where the two diagonal folds meet each other. *Drifter* now looks like the one shown in Illus. 44. Unfold the paper and turn it over. It should look like Illus. 45.

Notice the two arrows shown in Illus. 45. Take hold of the paper at the points indicated by the two arrows. Now you're holding the paper right on the fold line you made in Illus. 44.

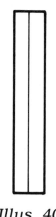

Illus. 40

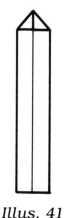

Illus. 41

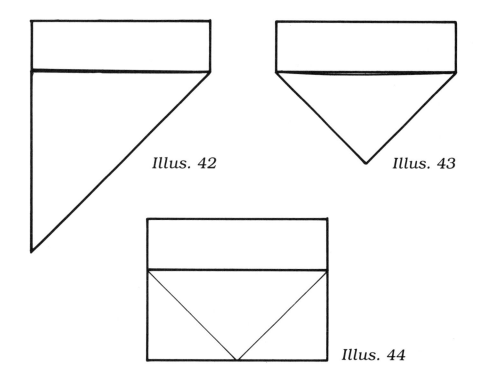

Illus. 42

Illus. 43

Illus. 44

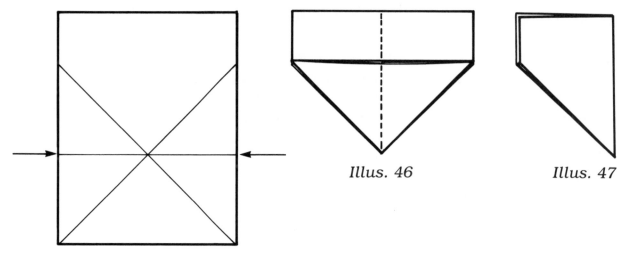

Illus. 45

Illus. 46

Illus. 47

Push in with both hands. Work the bottom edge of the paper upwards until the paper folds itself together, as shown in Illus. 46. You've just pushed the sides of the paper together. The dotted line down the middle of Illus. 46 indicates your next fold.

Illus. 47 shows how *Drifter* looks after making the fold shown in Illus. 46.

After creasing the middle fold, open *Drifter* again so it looks as it did in Illus. 46.

Slip the pointed end of the narrow strip of paper into the nose section of the airplane. Make sure that the middle fold of the narrow strip exactly matches the middle fold of the plane's body. Your project should now look like the drawing in Illus. 48.

Now turn your airplane over. Fold about one and one-half inches of the nose section back and crease it into place. This step is shown in Illus. 49.

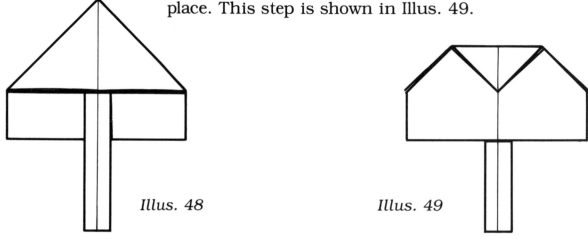

Illus. 48

Illus. 49

Turn the airplane over *again*. Fold down the right nose point, as shown in Illus. 50. This nose point is just two thicknesses of paper. Don't try to pull down the wing with the nose point. When you fold the other nose point into place, the result is shown in Illus. 51.

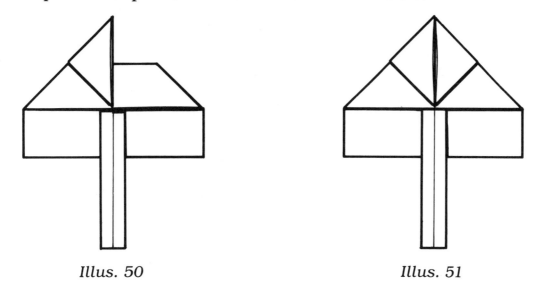

Illus. 50   Illus. 51

Now refold *Drifter* along its middle fold so the airplane looks like the one shown in Illus. 52. The dotted line indicates the wing fold you'll make after you strengthen the nose.

Before you make the wing folds, you must make *Drifter's* nose stronger. Otherwise, the nose might bend the first time *Drifter* makes a nose-first landing.

Cut a triangular piece of cereal-box material just large enough to fit into the airplane's pointed nose. In fact, cut *two* pieces from the cereal box: *Drifter* usually needs a bit of extra nose weight to give it perfect trim. To give the nose added strength, make these pieces long enough so that they extend back into the thick part of the nose. Illus. 53 shows *Drifter's* nose with the

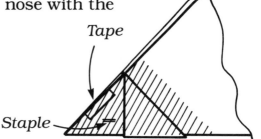

Illus. 53

Tape

Staple

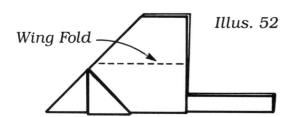

Wing Fold

Illus. 52

cardboard in place. The cardboard is shaded so that you can see it—even though it's out of sight when it's in place.

Slip the piece (or pieces) of cardboard between the two sides of *Drifter's* nose. Staple or glue them into place so that they don't slip out the first time *Drifter* crashes or lands hard. Wrap a strip of tape over the top of the airplane's nose as well. Now refer back to Illus. 52.

Fold down the wing nearer to you and crease the fold. Turn the airplane over and do the same for the other wing. As soon as you open its wings, *Drifter* is ready to be launched.

After a test flight or two, try bending the trailing edges of *Drifter's* wings up a bit. Remember how to roll the paper between your thumb and your fingers so it bends upwards in a gentle curve. This gives the airplane's wings more lift and it will help keep it in the air for longer flights.

Be careful not to staple your finger!

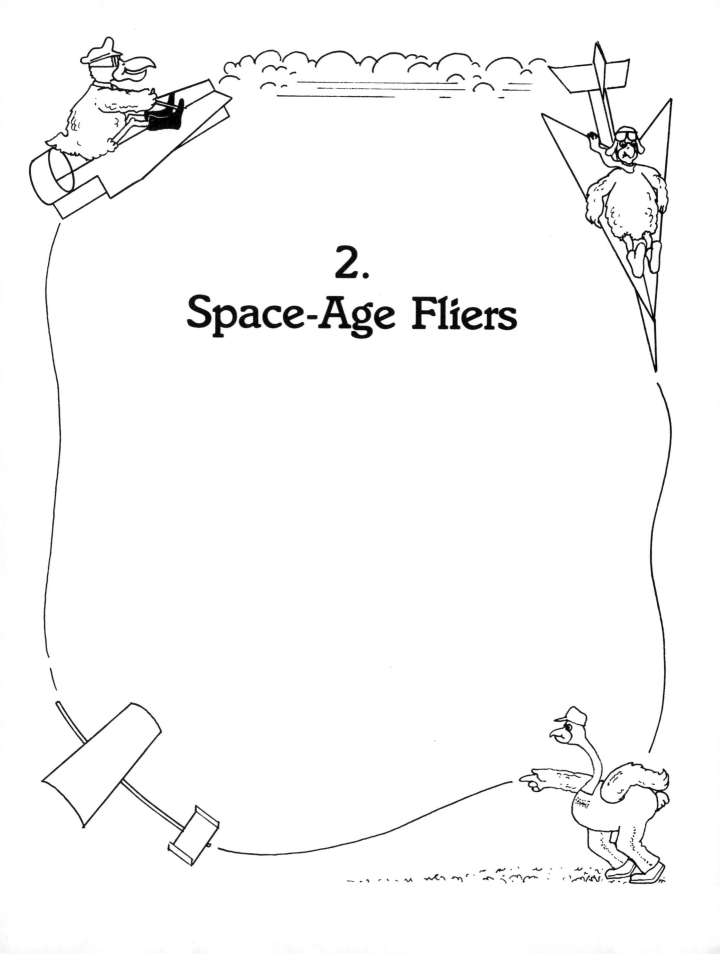

2.
Space-Age Fliers

Space-Age Fliers

The airplanes in this section all have designs reminding us of the shapes of the last thirty years—the Space Age.

Probe

Fold a sheet of notebook paper or typing paper in half the short way. Turn it so that the fold is towards you, as shown in Illus. 54.

While the paper is still folded, make the cut shown in the drawing. Hold the paper carefully so that the two sides don't slip when you're using the scissors. Make the cut at (about) the angle shown in the drawing. Stop cutting when you're one and one-quarter inches from the folded edge.

Illus. 55 shows four dotted lines where you'll make four folds. Fold the loose edges of the paper down towards you, one inch from the edge of the paper. Crease

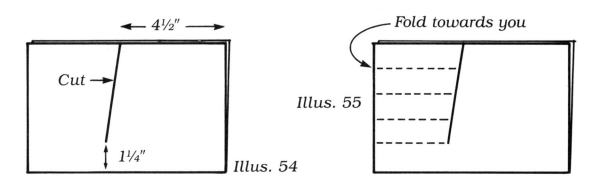

Illus. 55

Illus. 54

this fold firmly into place. Things should now look like the drawing shown in Illus. 56.

Fold the paper backwards for the next fold and crease the fold. You probably called this an "accordion" fold or a "fan" fold in your art class. Illus. 57 shows your progress.

One more forward fold and one more backward fold. This finishes this bit of folding. Your *Probe* looks like the one shown in Illus. 58.

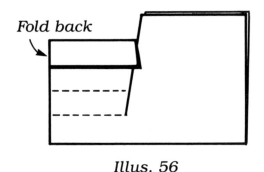

Fold back

Illus. 56

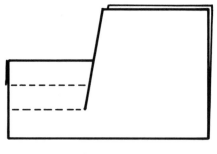

Illus. 57

Crease these folds tightly. A good way to do this is to press the back of your thumbnail down and pull it along the fold you want to crease. You could also pull a ruler along the fold while you hold the paper firmly. Press down on the ruler *hard.*

The two dotted lines on *Probe's* nose shown in Illus. 58 show where you're going to fold next. Make the first fold towards you and then crease it. Make the second fold *away* from you. This brings us to Illus. 59. Be sure to crease the last fold firmly. Be careful not to tear the paper.

Now wrap a strip of tape several times around *Probe's* nose as shown in Illus. 59. Add a strip of tape around the front of the airplane's nose, as well. Turn the paper over for just a minute and you'll see that the ends of the folded paper stick out along the fuselage. Place a strip of tape over these ends along the fuselage.

The dotted line in Illus. 60 shows where to fold down the wing. Begin by folding the wing nearer to you into place by following the dotted line. Turn *Probe* over and fold its other wing into place. Your newest paper airplane should look like the one shown in Illus. 61.

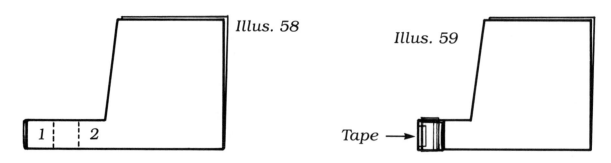

Illus. 58

Illus. 59

Tape →

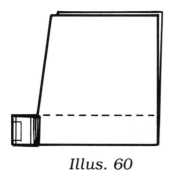

Illus. 60

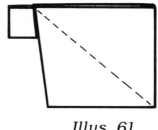

Illus. 61

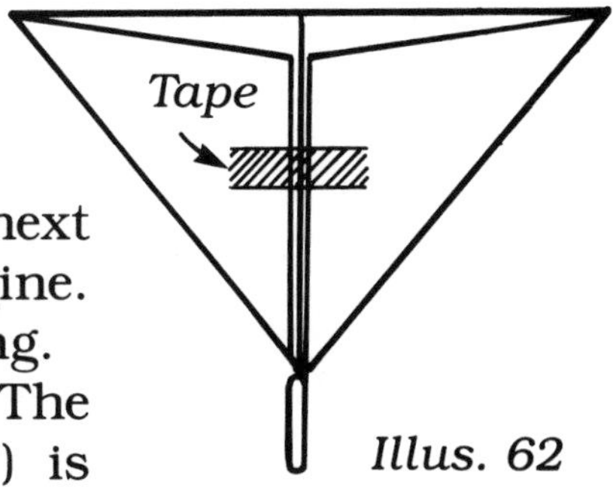

Illus. 62

The dotted line shown in Illus. 61 shows your next fold. Fold up the wing near you along the dotted line. Turn *Probe* over and do the same for the other wing.

Illus. 62 shows a top view of *Probe* at this stage. The shaded area in the drawing (marked as "tape") is shaded because after the tape is in place, you won't see much of it. Begin by making a little roll of tape with the sticky side out. This tape roll should be from one-quarter to three-eighths inch in diameter. Overlap one end of the tape onto the other to hold the little tape roll together.

Lift the top layers of the wings (you just folded the wings into place) just enough so that you can place the tape between the bottom and the top of each wing. Press the tape onto the bottom section of one side only!

Now press the top side of the wing onto the tape so that the bottom and the top of one wing are taped together. Don't let the tape touch the other wing yet!

Before you tape the second wing, look at Illus. 63, a front-on view of *Probe*. See how the wings tip downwards. This gives *Probe* a negative dihedral, or drooping wings.

When you press the top of the wing down onto the bottom part of the wing, the roll of tape is pressed together. Now it is a flattened piece of tape instead of a round roll of tape. One end is stuck between two sections of wing. The other end is sticking out ready for use.

Bend the end of the tape downwards. By bending it downwards, you'll give your wings a negative dihedral. Press the end of the tape onto the bottom of the second

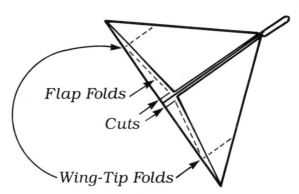

Illus. 64

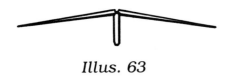

Illus. 63

Flap Folds

Cuts

Wing-Tip Folds

wing. Be sure to hold the fuselage together as you're doing this.

Check Illus. 63 to be sure you give *Probe's* wings the same sort of negative dihedral that is shown in the drawing.

Press the top of the second wing onto the sticky tape and *Probe's* wings are securely fastened into place.

Illus. 64 has two dotted lines to show you where to fold the airplane's wing tips upwards. Fold both wing tips so that they stand straight up and become vertical stabilizers.

Illus. 64 also shows two cut lines on either side of the fuselage. Make these cuts one-half inch deep. Fold the rear flaps upwards along the two dotted lines extending from the cuts to the wing-tip folds.

Once this cutting and folding is done, tear off a bit of tape. Fasten the two sides of the fuselage together at the very rear of the airplane. Just fold the tape around the end of the fuselage. Now *Probe* is ready for flying.

With all that folded paper and tape at its nose, *Probe* won't even need a paper clip for trim. By adjusting the angle of its rear control flaps you'll be able to make *Probe* glide in a long, straight path.

Try leaving one control flap down and bending the other up to put *Probe* into a turn.

If the airplane's fuselage (behind its nose) gets weak from too many landings, you can add a bit of tape to strengthen it. Or, just take a minute to build a new model.

Simplicity

Simplicity is an easy airplane to construct, and it has simple, pleasing lines. Once it is properly trimmed, *Simplicity* flies in a simple, absolutely fabulous long distance glide.

Start with a sheet of notebook paper or typing paper and fold the bottom edge upwards and towards the top along the dotted line shown in Illus. 65. This fold is about one-third of the way up from the bottom edge.

Turn the folded paper sideways and fold it down the middle as shown in Illus. 66. This fold gives you *Simplicity's* middle line.

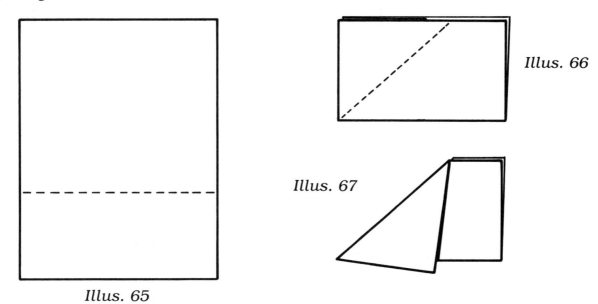

Illus. 66

Illus. 67

Illus. 65

The dotted line shown in Illus. 66 indicates your next fold. Check Illus. 67 before making this next fold. See how the fold brings the corner of the paper down about one-half inch below the airplane's middle line.

Fold the side nearer to you into position and then crease the fold. Turn the paper over and fold the second side into position so that both sides match. *Simplicity* should now look like Illus. 67.

Now we need to do a bit of taping. Begin by taping together the lower edges of the sides you just folded, as shown in Illus. 68. Then tape the side against the fuselage. This bit of tape is also shown in Illus. 68. Turn the airplane over and tape the other side against the fuselage.

Now it's time to do a bit of cutting. Hold *Simplicity's* two sides together as you make the cut shown in Illus. 68. This cut begins one inch from the rear of the airplane and is two inches long. The cut does not go straight down, but it's made at a bit of an angle.

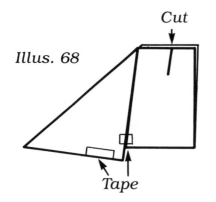

Illus. 68

Cut

Tape

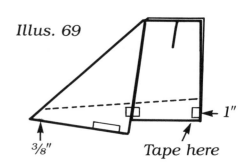

Illus. 69

1"

⅜"

Tape here

The dotted line shown in Illus. 69 shows your next fold. This fold runs at a bit of an angle from the nose to the tail. It starts about three-eighths inch above the middle fold at the nose and is one full inch above the middle fold by the time it gets to the tail. Be sure you make this fold at (about) the angle shown in the drawing.

Fold down the side nearer you and crease the fold. You've just made one of *Simplicity's* wings. Turn the airplane over and fold the second wing into place. It should match the first wing exactly.

Once the two wings are folded, press the sides of the fuselage together at the tail and fasten them together with a bit of cellophane tape or masking tape. The tape is shown by the arrow in Illus. 69.

Illus. 70 shows *Simplicity* viewed from the top. The two dotted lines show where to fold up the vertical stabilizers into position. Be careful with these folds! These folds are parallel with the center line of the airplane. This is important. Don't let these folds angle off—*Simplicity* won't perform well if you do.

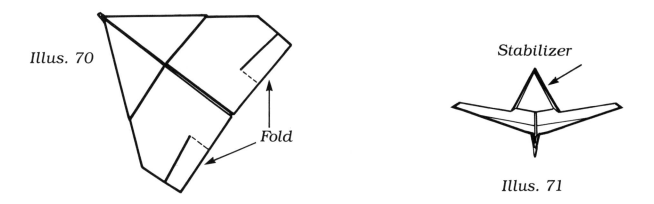

Illus. 70

Fold

Stabilizer

Illus. 71

Once the two stabilizers are folded upwards, it's time for the final bit of taping. Pull the tops of the two stabilizers together without bending them. Tape the two of them together so that the two vertical stabilizers now form one triangle-shaped stabilizer. At the same time, give the wings a bit of dihedral. Illus. 71 shows a front view of *Simplicity* ready to test-fly.

Quick! Get me another piece of tape!

Slip one paper clip onto *Simplicity*'s fuselage at its nose. Launch the airplane with a steady forward thrust with your arm and wrist. You should get a long, absolutely steady glide. If you need to work on the airplane's trim a bit, roll the trailing edges of both wings up slightly. Bend these control surfaces upwards just a tiny bit.

Once you get the right combination of paper clip at the nose and slightly upward-bent trailing edges, *Simplicity* will give you one of the greatest flights you've ever had with a paper airplane.

Lean and Mean

When *Lean and Mean* is finished and ready to fly, it has the appearance of a sleek spacecraft, ready to explore outer space.

Fold a sheet of notebook paper (or similar paper) in half the long way. Crease the fold, then open the paper out flat. Turn the paper over, so that the fold you just made stands up like a little ridge in the middle of your paper. Illus. 72 shows the middle fold already made. The two dotted lines indicate your next folds.

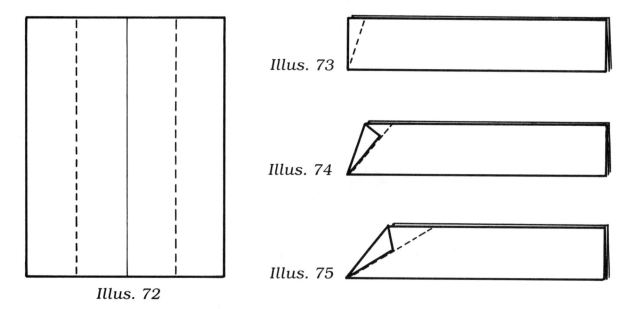

Illus. 72

Illus. 73

Illus. 74

Illus. 75

Fold the paper along the dotted lines so that both edges of the paper meet at the middle fold. Leave these folds in place.

Refold *Lean and Mean* along its middle fold. It now looks like the drawing shown in Illus. 73. The middle fold is at the bottom of the drawing. The dotted line in Illus. 73 shows your next fold.

Fold down the side nearer to you along the dotted line. You're folding two layers of paper at this point.

Turn the airplane over and fold the other side in exactly the same way. Once again, you're folding two layers of paper.

We're now at Illus. 74. The dotted line shows where to make the next fold.

Once again, fold the wing nearer you along the dotted line. Turn the paper over and fold the second wing to match the first.

After completing these folds you should be at the stage shown in Illus. 75.

There's another dotted line shown in Illus. 75. Make the fold shown by that dotted line. Just as you've been doing, fold the side nearer to you. Turn *Lean and Mean* over, and fold the other side in exactly the same manner.

Illus. 76 shows the airplane as it looks now. One arrow in the drawing points to a piece of cellophane tape or masking tape. Use a small piece of tape to fasten the folded layers flat against the wing, as shown in the drawing.

Illus. 76

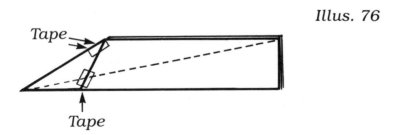

Tape

Tape

Turn the airplane over and tape the folded layers on the other side against the other wing in the same way.

Once this taping is done, pull the two wings together at the top. Fold a piece of tape over the tops of the wings to fasten them together. This is the tape shown by the two arrows in Illus. 76.

At this point, the tops of the two wings have become a long, narrow vertical stabilizer even though you can't see it quite yet.

The dotted line in Illus. 76 shows where to fold next. Fold the bottom of the wing nearer you upwards along the dotted line. Crease the fold well to hold it in place.

Turn *Lean and Mean* over and make the same fold on the other wing. When this is done your airplane should look like Illus. 77.

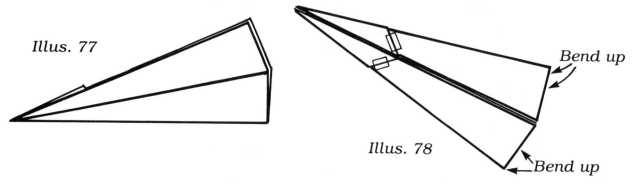

Illus. 77

Illus. 78

Bend up

Bend up

Now spread the wings you just folded upwards so that they stick out to the sides horizontally. Illus. 78 shows a top view of *Lean and Mean* with its wings outspread.

Bend up the trailing edges of the wings slightly at the points shown by the arrows in the drawing. Bend by rolling the paper between your thumb and fingers to give it a rounded bend.

Launch this paper airplane with a sharp, forward motion of your hand and arm.

It may fly perfectly the first time you launch it. If it stalls, try giving the trailing edges of the wings a bit less upward bend. Or, add a paper clip or even two to the airplane's nose.

If *Lean and Mean* dives, adjust the airplane's trim by giving it a bit more upward bend of the rear control surfaces. You're looking for a fast, straight flight from *Lean and Mean*.

But wait! *Lean and Mean* has one fabulous flight characteristic which it does not always display. Sometimes this airplane will suddenly twirl while in mid-flight. Sometimes it does a complete 360° spin about its middle fold without slowing down. It probably won't twirl on every flight, but it will do it sometimes.

If your *Lean and Mean* does not do this 360° twirl for you, adjust the trim so that it flies in a perfectly straight, flat, fast glide. Bend up one aileron on a trailing edge slightly than the other one, then fly the airplane again.

Be careful when you adjust the trim of *Lean and Mean* to make it spin in flight. Too much upward bending of a control surface will cause the airplane to bank or turn to one side or the other. It may twirl even when it is banking.

If you're lucky, and if *Lean and Mean* cooperates, you'll get two 360° spins in the same flight.

Lunar Lander

Astronauts want a space lander to be steady and to have a smooth glide path. *Lunar Lander* gives you exactly those flight characteristics.

Fold your sheet of notebook paper or typing paper in half the short way. Illus. 79 shows the paper with this fold already in place. The dotted line shows you where to make the next fold.

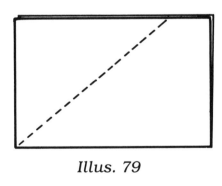

Illus. 79

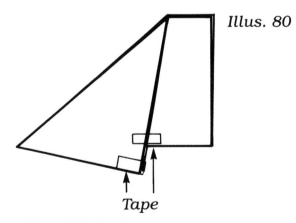

Illus. 80

Tape

Before making this next fold, look at Illus. 80. In this drawing, the fold has been made so that the folded corner extends down one inch past the paper's middle fold.

Now fold down the wing nearer you along the dotted line as shown in Illus. 79. Turn the paper over and fold the other wing to match the first. Be sure the tips of these wings stick down one inch lower than the paper's middle fold.

Do some taping before going on. Tape the two wing tips together, as shown in Illus. 80.

Now tape each wing against the fuselage, as shown in Illus. 80. Make sure you place this bit of tape just above the middle fold, and not much higher. When you fold the wing into place, you don't want the tape to get in your way.

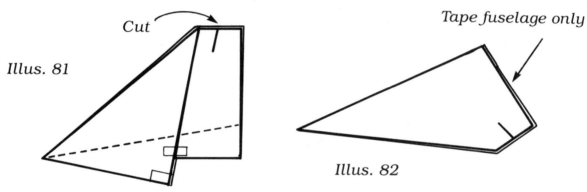

Illus. 81

Cut

Tape fuselage only

Illus. 82

Move on to Illus. 81. Hold the two halves of the paper tightly together when you make the cut shown. It should be one and one-half inches from the rear of the airplane. It should be just a little more than one inch long.

After making this cut, it's time to fold down the wings into place. The dotted line shown in Illus. 81 shows where to make this fold.

Fold down the wing nearer to you and crease the fold. Turn the airplane over and fold down the other wing to match. After folding the wings down, tape both sides of the rear of the fuselage together: Illus. 82 shows where.

Once the fuselage is taped, it's time to fold the vertical stabilizers into place. Illus. 83 shows a top view of *Lunar Lander*. Fold the stabilizers up along the dotted lines in the illustration. Be sure you make these folds so the stabilizers are perfectly parallel to the middle fold of the airplane. You can see that the dotted fold lines are parallel to the middle line of *Lunar Lander*.

Once the vertical stabilizers are folded up and into place, slip two paper clips onto *Lunar Lander's* nose, as shown in Illus. 83.

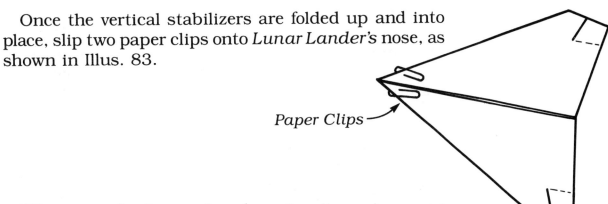

Paper Clips

Illus. 83

When you fly *Lunar Lander*, give it a nice, even launching and it should go into a steady, even glide.

If you find you need only one paper clip, remove the two you have in place and slip one onto the nose of the fuselage, right under the leading edges of the wings.

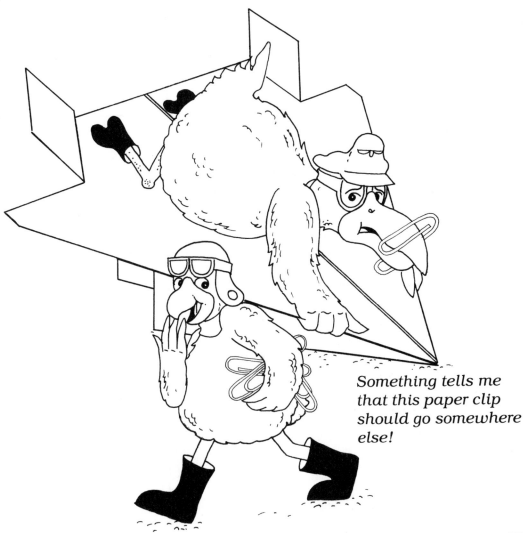

Something tells me that this paper clip should go somewhere else!

Shuttle

This little *Shuttle* is just the thing for quick trips. It has a snappy glide path and, sometimes it finishes its flight by "showing off" with a 360° spin, or a roll just before it lands.

Begin by folding your sheet of notebook paper or other paper in half the short way. Illus. 84 shows this fold in place. The next fold (along the dotted line) is also shown in Illus. 84.

After making this last fold, unfold the paper so it looks like the sheet shown in Illus. 85. The two dotted lines shown in this drawing indicate your next folds.

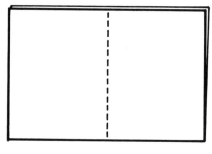

Illus. 84

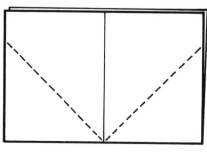

Illus. 85

Once these folds are made, things look like the drawing shown in Illus. 86. Now unfold the two folds you just made so you're back to where you were at Illus. 85.

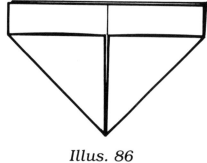

Illus. 86

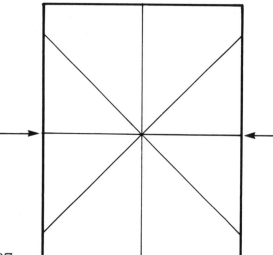

Illus. 87

Turn the paper over and refold the two diagonal folds. You should make these folds limber enough to make the next folding steps easy.

Once you've done this reverse folding, unfold the entire paper and flatten it out so it looks like the one shown in Illus. 87.

Take hold of the paper at the two points shown by the arrows in Illus. 87. Push your hands towards each other and wiggle the paper a bit so that the two sides slip inside the paper as the ends fold over. When you are finished you have arrived at Illus. 88.

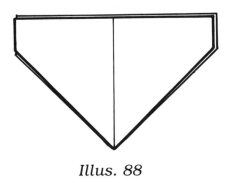

Illus. 88

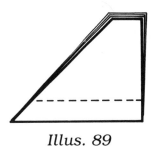

Illus. 89

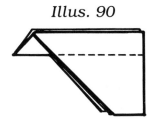

Illus. 90

Fold *Shuttle* along the middle fold (already in place) and *Shuttle* looks like the drawing in Illus. 89.

The dotted line shown in Illus. 89 indicates the first wing fold. Fold down the wing nearer to you along the dotted line. When you do this, you're folding down two layers of paper. Now turn the airplane over and fold the other wing so it matches the first one. With these two folds made, you've reached the point shown in Illus. 90.

The dotted line shown in this drawing shows your next fold. Fold up *only* the top section of paper when you make the fold shown in Illus. 90.

Turn the airplane over and do the same for the other wing. You're folding up only the *top* section of each wing along the dotted line. With this folding finished, your *Shuttle* looks like the drawing shown in Illus. 91.

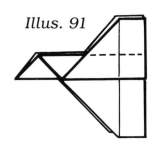

Illus. 91

The dotted line shown in Illus. 91 shows your next fold. Fold down the nearer side along the dotted line, then turn the airplane over and make the same fold on the other side. You're at Illus. 92 now.

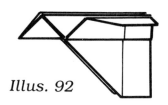

Illus. 92

Lift up the two ends you just folded so that they look as they did in Illus. 91. Check Illus. 93 to be sure you've folded this correctly.

Tape together the two tips you just unfolded, as shown with the single arrow shown in Illus. 93.

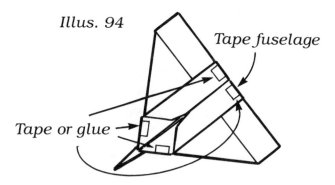

Illus. 94

Tape fuselage

Tape or glue

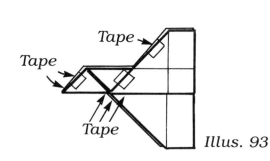

Tape

Tape

Tape

Illus. 93

Tape the fuselage nose together. This strip of tape is shown with double arrows shown in the drawing in Illus. 93.

Finally, add the strip of tape shown with triple arrows. Turn the airplane over and add a similar bit of tape to the other side.

Take hold of the fuselage with one hand and lift the wings with the other. The area where you applied the first strip of tape now forms the vertical stabilizer. Illus. 94 is a top view of shuttle.

Tape the rear of the fuselage together. You can't see where that tape goes, but the arrow shows where it should go.

You can either put on the four little bits of tape as shown in Illus. 94, or you can glue the top layer of the wing to the bottom layer. I used tape but glue works just fine. The important thing is to make sure the top layer of wing is held tightly to the bottom layer of wing.

Slip a paper clip onto the fuselage nose and test-fly your *Shuttle*. It may need two paper clips for proper trim. Experiment with bending the two trailing edges upwards to give more lift.

When your *Shuttle* is trimmed, it should give you a 360° roll at the end of a few of its flights. If it doesn't, experiment with bending up one wing flap slightly more than the other. That should do the job.

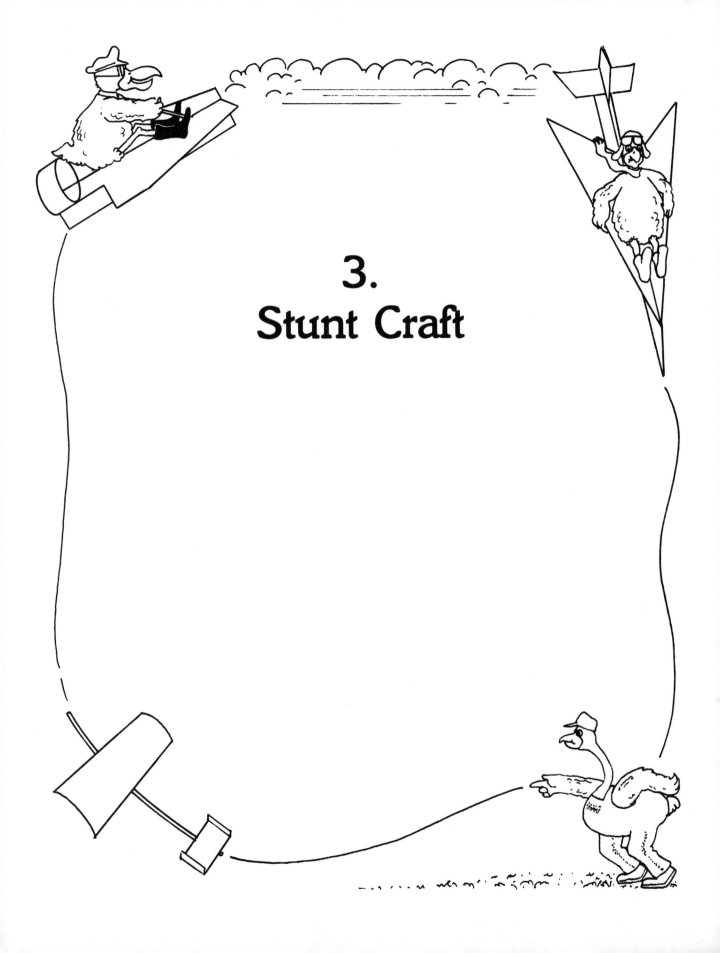

3.
Stunt Craft

Stunt Craft

All of the paper airplanes in this section can do a bit of trick flying and stunt flying. Mostly it's a matter of proper trim and learning how to launch them.

Loop de Loop

Loop de Loop is very easy to construct. It's also a fabulous stunt flier.

Begin by folding a sheet of notebook paper or typing paper in half the short way. After creasing the fold, unfold the paper so that it looks like the drawing shown in Illus. 95. The fold you just made is a measuring line. We'll use this line in just a minute. The dotted line shown in Illus. 95 shows your first fold.

After making the first fold, *Loop de Loop* should look like the drawing shown in Illus. 96. Make the fold shown by the dotted line in Illus. 96.

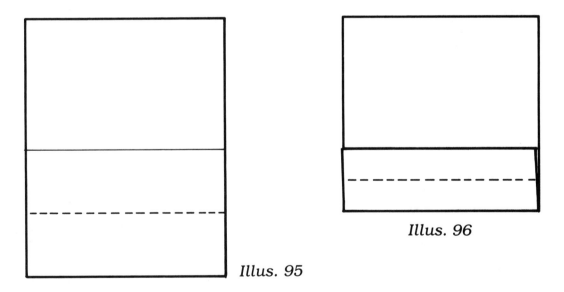

Illus. 96

Illus. 95

With that fold in place, your airplane should look like Illus. 97. Fold along the dotted line in that drawing, and crease down the thick layers of paper tightly. Use your thumbnail, or a ruler, or even the side of a pencil to press these folds tightly into place.

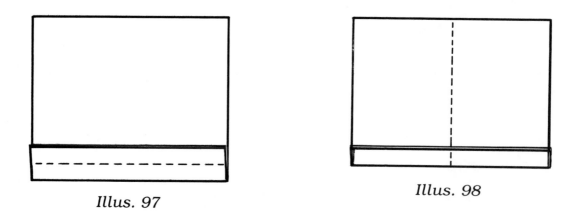

Illus. 97

Illus. 98

Illus. 98 shows your airplane with the nose folds all done. the dotted line indicates the next fold. Turn the sheet as shown in the drawing.

With the middle fold in place, it's time to use scissors. Illus. 99 shows how *Loop de Loop* looks after the last fold. The drawing also shows where you're going to cut out a section of the airplane.

Measure up three-quarters inch from the middle fold and make the first cut. This cut is exactly two inches

Careful with that iron, bud. You don't want to burn yourself!

long. Be sure this cut is parallel to the middle fold and don't let the two sides of the airplane slip as you cut. Make the second cut; it runs down from the edge of the wing to the cut you just made.

Once these two cuts are made, your airplane looks like the one shown in Illus. 100. The dotted line shown in Illus. 100 indicates the wing fold.

Fold the wing nearer to you, then turn the airplane over and fold the other wing down, so that it matches the first.

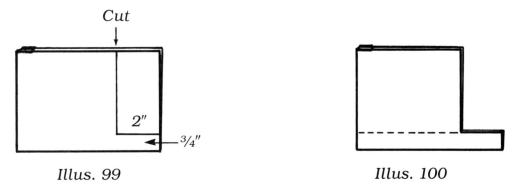

Illus. 99   *Illus. 100*

Unfold the airplane as shown in Illus. 101. This is a top view of *Loop de Loop.*

Bend the trailing edges of the wings up at the points indicated by the arrows in Illus. 101. Make sure the wings have a little dihedral—your first stunt flier is now ready for launching.

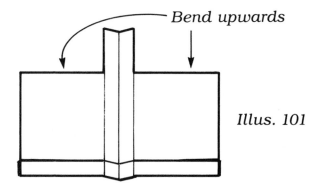

Illus. 101

Point the nose of *Loop de Loop* down slightly and launch it with a fast snap of your arm and wrist.

This fabulous little stunt plane should perform a loop for you. By experimenting with the trailing edges of the wings, you can make this little aircraft bank to either side after it comes out of its loop. In fact, you can even persuade it to bank *during* its loop.

Sleek

We think of "sleek" airplanes as those having a stream-lined appearance. *Sleek* has an appearance all its own, and it can also do some fancy stunt flying.

Begin by making the fold shown by the dotted line shown in Illus. 102. Make certain this fold is exactly one and one-half inches from the bottom of the paper. Crease the fold carefully so that the folded paper lies completely flat.

Check Illus. 103. It shows the first fold already in place. This drawing also shows three more folds just like the one you already finished.

To make each of these folds, just fold the inch and one-half section over and crease the fold carefully. By the time you make the final fold you will have folded the paper four times.

Illus. 102

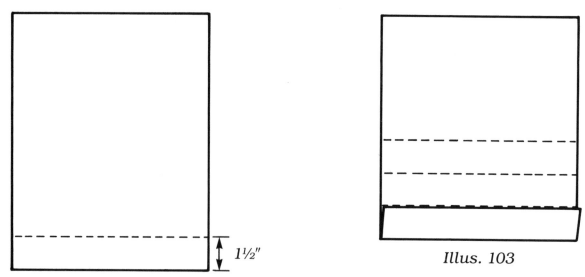

1½″

Illus. 103

When all four folds are finished and creased, place the paper on the desk so that the folded layers are underneath the main part of the (future) paper airplane. Illus. 104 shows this step.

The dotted line shown in Illus. 104 indicates your next fold. This fold comes three-quarters of an inch from the bottom of the paper. What this means, of course, is that with this fold, you fold all those layers of paper exactly in half. Make this fold carefully and crease it firmly into place.

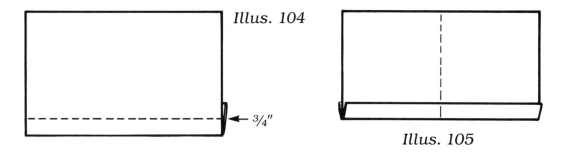

Illus. 104

Illus. 105

Sleek now looks like the drawing shown in Illus. 105. The dotted line in the drawing shows the middle fold. Fold the middle fold next.

After making *Sleek's* middle fold, it should look like Illus. 106. The dotted line in this illustration shows your next fold.

Note that this fold begins just to the right of that thick layer of folded paper. Fold the paper towards you along the dotted line. Then, fold the paper away from you along the fold you just made. This makes it easy to accomplish the next step.

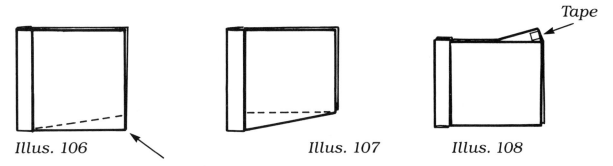

Tape

Illus. 106   *Illus. 107*   *Illus. 108*

The arrow in Illus. 106 shows where to push up and in on the paper you just folded back and forth. Use one finger to push this folded paper so it turns itself inside out. When you finish, this long, narrow triangle of paper is now inside the airplane—it will become *Sleek's* vertical stabilizer.

Illus. 107 shows *Sleek* after this folding and pushing. The wing fold (indicated by the dotted line) comes next.

Fold down the wing nearer to you along the dotted line and then crease the fold. Turn the airplane over and fold the second wing so that it matches the first. *Sleek* should now look like Illus. 108.

Use a small piece of cellophane tape to fasten together the two sides of the vertical stabilizer. Illus. 108 shows the tape's location.

Open the wings so the airplane looks like the drawing shown in Illus. 109. Check the two dotted lines—they show where to fold up the wing tips to make vertical stabilizers at the end of each wing.

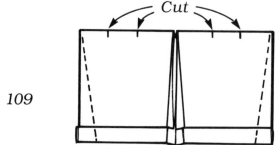

Illus. 109

At the trailing edge of each wing you'll see two cuts. Make these cuts one-quarter inch deep. Now you can fold up the trailing edge between each pair of cuts to make control surfaces.

Before launching *Sleek*, give its wings a bit of a curve by pushing down with your thumbs on the leading edges of its wings. While you push down with your thumbs, support the bottom side of the wings with your fingers. Don't fold the wings when you do this. Just rub your thumbs back and forth over the thick folds of paper at the leading edges and put a bit of a curve in the wings.

To launch *Sleek*, give it a snap of your wrist. With all that folded paper up front you won't have to worry about adding any weight for trim—it's already there.

If *Sleek* dives, bend up the two ailerons you made in the trailing edges of its wings. Once you have *Sleek* trimmed, it will perform inside loops for you. If you aim the airplane downwards when you launch it, *Sleek* will do an immediate loop.

Perfect

Perfect gets it name from its perfect glide path. With slight modification, *Perfect* becomes a great stunt plane. *Perfect* is also easy to fold.

Begin by folding your notebook paper (or other paper) down the middle the long way. Unfold it and lay it flat, as shown. in Illus. 110.

The two dotted lines in Illus. 110 show where you'll fold the paper next. Fold each corner right to the middle line. Your sheet should now look just like the drawing shown in Illus. 111.

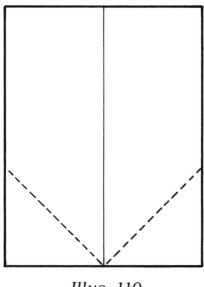

Illus. 110

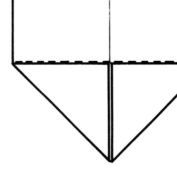

Illus. 111

The dotted line shown in Illus. 111 is your next fold. After making this fold, your airplane should look like Illus. 112. The two dotted lines in this drawing show your next folds.

When you make these folds, the corners of the paper should come together exactly at the middle line. Illus. 113 shows how things should look once these folds have been made.

Hey, big guy—think you're perfect, or what?

Now make the fold along the dotted line shown in Illus. 113. When this fold is made, fold *Perfect* along its middle line—it should look exactly like the drawing shown in Illus. 114.

The dotted line shown in Illus. 114 indicates where to make *Perfect's* wing folds.

Fold down the wing nearer you along the dotted line. Turn the airplane over and fold down the second wing so it matches the first.

Perfect is now ready for testing. Make sure its wings extend out horizontally or with just a slight bit of dihedral. Give *Perfect* a nice, steady launch. When you

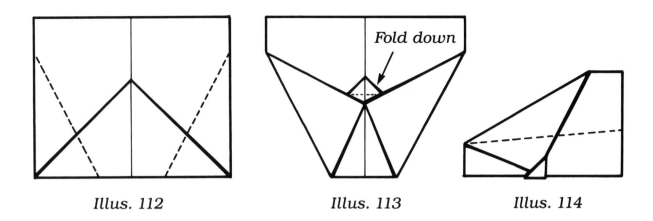

Illus. 112   Illus. 113   Illus. 114

launch *Perfect* straight forward with a smooth motion, it should perform a nice, steady glide for you.

Let's see what stunts *Perfect* can do. Bend the trailing edges of its wings upwards a bit—*Perfect* will do better at stunt flying.

First, launch *Perfect* almost straight up into the air with a quick snap of your arm and wrist. Unless you're in a room with a very high ceiling, go outdoors for this launching. *Perfect* should do a loop overhead when launched upwards like this.

Hold *Perfect* so that the underside of the fuselage is towards you. With its nose pointed up and at a little angle away from you, give *Perfect* a quick upward snap of your arm and wrist. When launched like this, *Perfect* should do a nice inside loop and come back towards you.

With a little experimenting, you'll get *Perfect* to do a circle after making a loop in the air. Just have a little patience and get the training edges of its wings bent into the right position.

Let's do one final experiment with *Perfect.* Fold the trailing edges of both wings straight down. Start this fold at the edge of the fuselage and let it extend down the sides of the wings for one and one-quarter inches. The dotted lines in Illus. 115 show where to make this fold.

With these control surfaces folded down, launch *Perfect* with a quick snap of your wrist as though you were sending the airplane on a long flight. If the control flaps are bent down properly, *Perfect* will fly out just a few feet and immediately go into an outside loop. This loop will bring *Perfect* right back to your feet.

Experiment until *Perfect* does this outside loop and then see how much of the loop your airplane will complete. Because it is impossible to give *Perfect* enough thrust, you'll never get it to totally complete its outside loop—at least I can't.

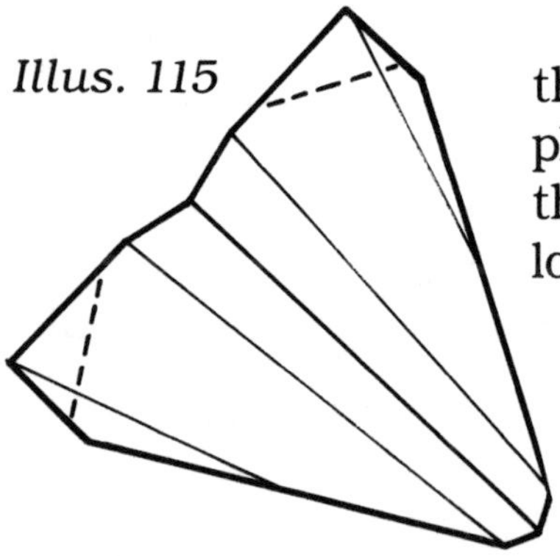

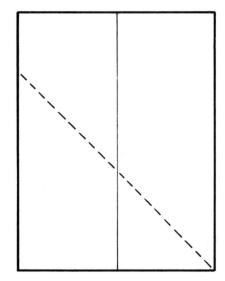

Illus. 115

Fancy

Fancy lives up to its name because of its many complicated-looking folds. When *Fancy* flies, it does such a nice job that there's never any question why it has its name.

Fold your paper in half the long way and then flatten it out so that it looks like Illus. 116.

Make the fold shown by the dotted line as seen in Illus. 116. Once your make this fold, unfold the paper.

Fancy now looks like the paper shown in Illus. 117. The dotted line in that drawing shows where to make your next fold. Make that fold, then unfold your paper once again.

Illus. 116

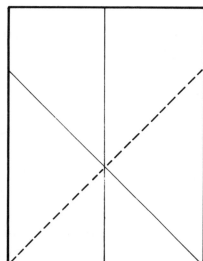

Illus. 117

With these folds in place, things look like the drawing shown in Illus. 118. The dotted line in this drawing indicates your next fold. Once again, make this fold, then unfold the paper.

Now push in on both edges at the points shown by the arrows in Illus. 118. Work the sides inwards so that the rest of the paper folds itself into the shape you see in Illus. 119.

Here come the tricky folds. Don't fold these until you're absolutely sure that you understand the instructions.

The dotted lines shown in Illus. 119 indicate this pair of folds. These folds are made only on the *bottom* layer of the airplane. This is why the dotted lines are dark at the top and then get lighter. The lighter parts of the dotted lines indicates that the folds are only on the bottom layer. The top layer stays unfolded.

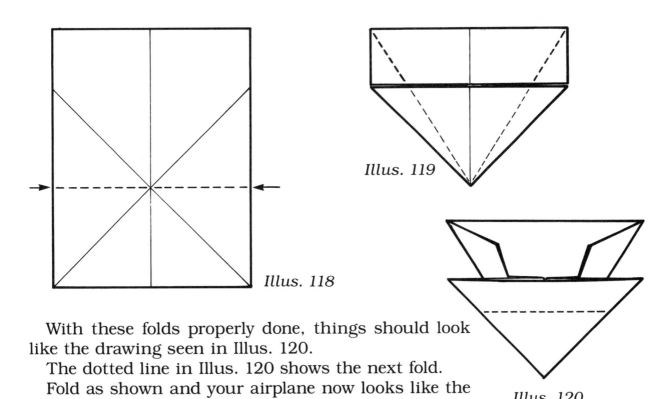

Illus. 119

Illus. 118

Illus. 120

With these folds properly done, things should look like the drawing seen in Illus. 120.

The dotted line in Illus. 120 shows the next fold.

Fold as shown and your airplane now looks like the drawing in Illus. 121. Fold down the point of paper along the dotted line shown in Illus. 121. Make sure the pointed end of the paper does not extend below the rest of the airplane.

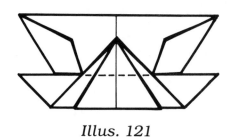

Illus. 121

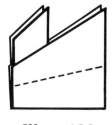

Illus. 122

Now fold *Fancy* along the middle line so it looks like the drawing shown in Illus. 122.

Hang on to your hat, buddy, it's going to be a fancy flight!

The dotted line in Illus. 122 shows where to make *Fancy's* wing folds. Fold down the wing nearer to you along that dotted line and crease the fold. Turn the airplane over and fold down the other wing into place.

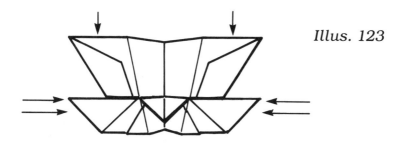

Illus. 123

Illus. 123 shows a top view of *Fancy* when it's completed. Its fuselage is spread so you can see all the various layers of paper created by your folding. Now let's have some flying fun.

Launch *Fancy* straight forward and you'll probably get a good glide. Dont' be surprised if *Fancy* banks near the end of the flight and tries to circle around to come back towards you.

Curl up or bend up the trailing edges of both wings (marked by single arrows in Illus. 123) and *Fancy* will do a great inside loop.

Try curling up the points of the front wing sections to see how this makes *Fancy's* flight path steadier. These wing points are marked by double arrows in Illus. 123.

Experiment with one trailing edge bent or curled higher than the other to get *Fancy* to bank and turn for you.

Curl one of the front wing's points higher than the other to make *Fancy's* flight path change.

It's fine to test *Fancy* in the house, but for this grand little airplane to really do its stuff, go to the gym or go outdoors. This little craft really gets out and flies.

Trickster

Trickster takes only about a minute to make. It will give you lots of fun as a stunt flier.

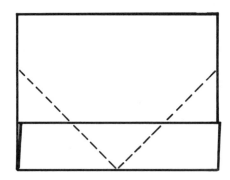

Illus. 124

Begin by turning your rectangular sheet of notebook paper or typing paper into a square sheet of paper. In case you've forgotten how to do this, turn back to the instructions on pages 5 and 6.

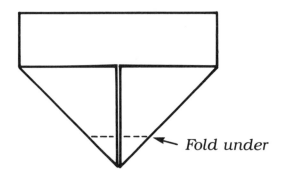

Illus. 125

← *Fold under*

Fold up the bottom two inches of your paper up so that it looks like the drawing shown in Illus. 124.

The two dotted lines in Illus. 124 show where you'll make your next folds. After making these two folds

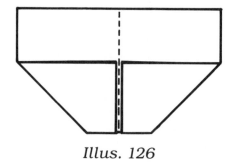

Illus. 126

your *Trickster* should look just like Illus. 125. The dotted line in the drawing shows your next fold.

Illus. 126 shows your paper airplane with the nose fold already in place. The dotted line down the middle indicates the next fold. After making the middle fold, *Trickster* is shown in Illus. 127. The dotted line in this drawing shows where you'll be folding *Trickster's* wings into place.

Fold down the wing which is closer to you into place along the dotted line. Finish by folding down the second wing so it matches the first.

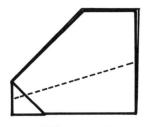

Illus. 127

Illus. 128 gives a bird's-eye view of the completed *Trickster.* Fold the trailing edges of its wings upwards. The arrows point to the spots to bend.

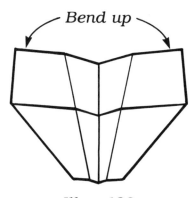

Illus. 128

Hold *Trickster* by its fuselage so its nose points straight upwards, as shown in Illus. 129. Launch the airplane with a rapid upward movement of your hand and arm.

When launched this way, *Trickster* should perform a great overhead loop and return to land fairly close to the point of takeoff.

You can adjust the size of *Trickster's* loops by the amount of bend or curl you put into the trailing edges of its wings.

Illus. 129

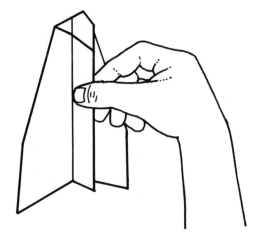

Of course you can straighten out those trailing edges and let *Trickster* become a level flier. Or, straighten out just *one* control surface and you'll send *Trickster* into a banking turn.

4.
Stepping Through
the Air

Stepping Through the Air

The fabulous paper airplanes in this section all have one thing in common: They all fly through the air in what looks like a series of little downward steps.

These airplanes don't go into long, smooth glides. They aren't fast fliers. They don't do lots of loops and rolls and other stunts.

They *will* give you a flight during which they seem to keep taking steps downwards as they travel through the air.

Little Dipper

You'll see why this little airplane is called *Little Dipper* as soon as you make it and take it on its first flight.

Cut a sheet of paper five inches wide by eleven and one-half inches long. Use a sheet of typing paper five inches wide and it will be the right length.

The dotted line in Illus. 130 shows your first fold. In order to make this fold correctly, you need to measure things first. Measure up from the bottom of the paper, along the left side, one and one-half inches. Mark that point with a dot.

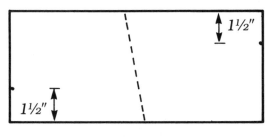

Illus. 130

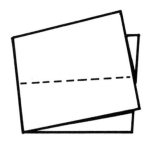

Illus. 131

Now measure down along the right side of the paper one and one-half inches from the top. Mark that point with a dot. Check Illus. 130 to make certain you've got the dots in the right places.

When you fold the paper, bring the right side over to the left. Place the dots on top of one another and crease the fold. With the fold made, *Little Dipper* looks like Illus. 131.

The dotted line in Illus. 131 shows how to make the next fold. You're going to fold the airplane in half right down its middle. Check the dotted line carefully, then make the fold.

Once you've folded the airplane in half, it should look like Illus. 132.

Before folding along the dotted line in Illus. 132, measure along the top of the paper. Measure two inches from the upper right-hand corner and place a dot there. Check the drawing shown in Illus. 132 to be sure that the dot is in the right place.

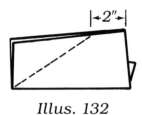

Illus. 132

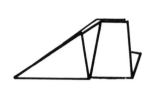

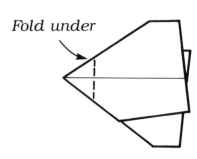

Fold under

Illus. 133 shows two views of the folded airplane at this stage—folded and unfolded.

Now fold down the wing nearer to you along the dotted line shown in Illus. 132. Bring the corner of the paper down so that it comes right to the middle fold.

Turn the airplane over and fold the other wing in exactly the same manner. *Little Dipper* is shown in Illus. 133 after making these folds.

Flatten the airplane out by unfolding the middle fold. It looks like the second drawing shown in Illus. 133.

Fold the nose down and under the rest of the airplane. The dotted line shown in the second part of Illus. 133 shows this fold.

Once the nose is folded under, *Little Dipper* looks just like the drawing shown in Illus. 134.

To launch *Little Dipper*, take hold of it by the rear of its middle fold. Place your index finger on top of the

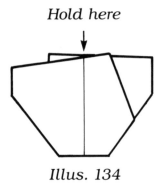

Hold here

Illus. 134

middle fold and place your thumb and your middle finger under it. Give *Little Dipper* a gentle push and set it free.

When this fabulous little paper airplane dips and steps its way through the air, you'll see the reason for its name. It takes short, gentle flights, with several little dips in each flight.

Experiment with *Little Dipper's* tail points. Bend or curl them so that they become control surfaces. Do the same with the trailing edges of its wings.

You can make its dips or steps shorter and you can get *Little Dipper* to bank and turn for you. This airplane refuses to glide in a long, level glide. Nor will it fly at great speed. *Little Dipper* just isn't that sort of airplane.

Wing

Once it is folded and ready for action, *Wing* does a fabulous job of stepping through the air. When most people look at *Wing*, they insist that it can't fly, but *Wing* surprises them every time.

Turn your sheet of notebook paper or typing paper so that the long edge is nearer you. Begin by making the fold shown by the dotted line in Illus. 135.

Illus. 136

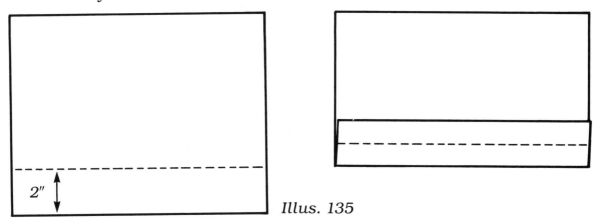

2"

Illus. 135

The width of this fold is *two inches*. Try to make this fold *exactly* two inches from the paper's bottom edge.

After this first fold is completed, *Wing* should look like Illus. 136. Make the next fold on the dotted line.

Now you're folding the first two-inch fold of paper in half.

Once this fold is finished, *Wing* should look just like Illus. 137. The final fold is indicated by the dotted line shown in the drawing. Fold the four thicknesses of paper over one more time.

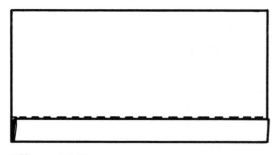

Illus. 137

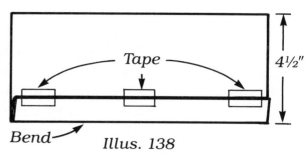

Illus. 138

When the last fold is made, your airplane should look like the drawing shown in Illus. 138. *Wing* is now about four and one-half inches from front to back.

Tape the folded leading edge of the wing down using three short strips of cellophane tape, or masking tape, as shown in Illus. 138.

Now bend *Wing* in the middle, at the point indicated by the arrow shown in Illus. 138. The key word is *bend*. Just bend the middle of the leading edge of the wing. You're not making a fold. The idea is just to put a bit of a bend in the leading edge to give *Wing* a little stability when it flies.

Wing needs a couple of control surfaces on its trailing edge. Check Illus. 139 to see where to make four scissor cuts. Make each of these cuts about one-fourth inch deep.

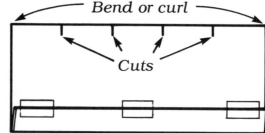

Illus. 139

When the cuts are made, bend up the two control flaps so that they're at about a 45° angle. This is halfway towards standing straight up.

Let's see how *Wing* behaves in the air. To launch this paper airplane, grasp it just as you did *Little Dipper*, with your forefinger on top of the rear of the wing and your thumb and your middle finger under the wing. Give it a gentle push into the air. It should do a fabulous job of stepping its way through the air across the room.

Wing reacts to air currents, as you'll soon see. You'll discover it will fly one way but not another, just because of the air currents. Adjust the flaps on the trailing edges to get the best flight. *Wing* may fly in a series of little dips and steps or it may glide smoothly across the room. It all depends upon your trailing-edge flaps and how the air is moving.

Experiment with a pair of paper clips on the leading edge of the wing; they might give you a longer flight.

If your plane reacts well to two paper clips, try four. They will make a definite difference in its flight characteristics.

After experimenting with more or less bending of the trailing edges, give *Wing* much more dihedral angle by folding a center fold into place. Just bring the wing tips together and crease the center. Then open *Wing* and it's ready to fly again. A front view of the folded wing is seen in Illus. 140. Test *Wing* with this middle fold in place.

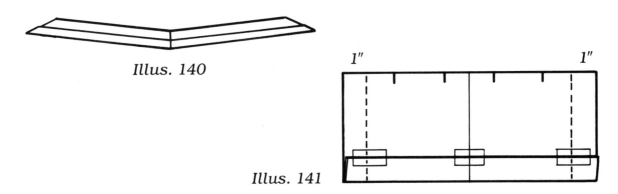

Illus. 140

Illus. 141

For *Wing's* last, and maybe its best performance, fold up both wing tips, as shown by the dotted lines in Illus. 141. These folds should each be one inch from the tip of each wing.

Crease these folds carefully and make sure both wing tips are standing straight up from the wing. Now they're vertical stabilizers; they'll make a real difference in the way *Wing* performs.

Launch your altered *Wing* as you did before. This time it will continue to step through the air, except that these steps will be longer than they were before. If *Wing* catches the right air current, its steps downwards will come far enough apart so that *Wing* appears to be on a glide path. Don't be surprised to get flights of twenty-five or thirty feet out of *Wing* when it is folded and trimmed in this manner.

Cruiser

You'll need a square piece of paper to construct *Cruiser*. Check pages 5 and 6 if you've forgotten how to make a rectangular sheet of paper into a square sheet.

Fold one corner over to the opposite corner and crease the fold. Unfold the paper. The fold line is shown in Illus. 142. The dotted line shown in the drawing indicates your next fold.

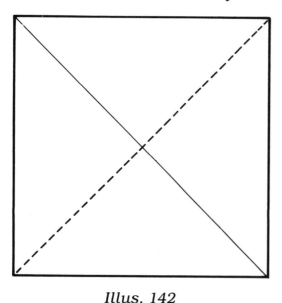

Illus. 142

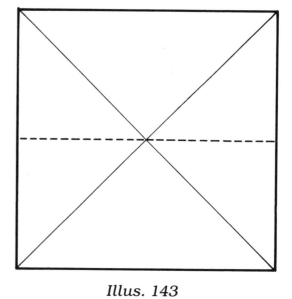

Illus. 143

Make the second fold and crease it; unfold the paper again. Your airplane is shown in Illus. 143 with both folds in place. The dotted line tells where to make your next fold. Make this fold, crease it, and then unfold the paper one more time.

Before folding again, refold the middle fold, but this time fold it in the direction opposite from the fold you just made. This will make the fold limber and it will be easy for you to complete your next step.

Need an extra hand folding Cruiser?

Help!

The two arrows shown in Illus. 144 show you where to push in from the sides of the paper. As you push your two hands together, the airplane folds in on itself. It should look just like Illus. 145 when this step is completed.

Check Illus. 145 for the cut you're going to make now. This cut has to be made *exactly* along the middle of your *Cruiser*. To find the middle, pull the wing tips together. Don't fold the airplane along the middle because you don't want it to have a middle fold when it's finished. Pull the wing tips together and then pinch a little fold in the paper right in the middle. This is where you will cut. Make this cut one and one-quarter inches long.

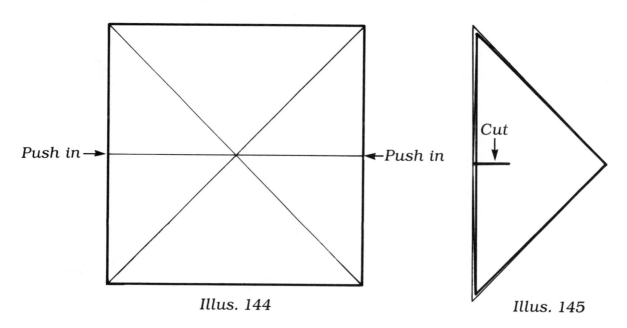

Illus. 144

Illus. 145

Now it's time to make the two folds indicated by the dotted lines shown in Illus. 146. Fold over all four layers of paper so that they lie flat on *Cruiser's* wing. Illus. 147 shows the folds in place. Fasten these layers down with two small strips of tape. The tape strips are also shown in Illus. 147.

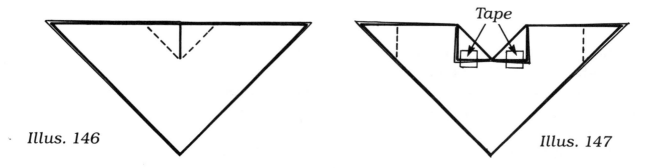

Illus. 146

Illus. 147

The two dotted lines in Illus. 147 show where to make your next folds, but don't fold yet. Fold only the top section of the wing upwards. The wing is now in two layers. Only the top layer is folded up. Make this fold one and one-half inches from the wing tip.

When these wing folds are in place, *Cruiser* should look just like the drawing shown in Illus. 148.

Use two small bits of tape to fasten both wing layers together. Illus. 148 shows where to put the tape.

Cruiser is about ready to take its first test flight. First, roll up the rear control surfaces as shown in Illus. 148. The arrows in the drawing show you where to roll or bend up four rear flaps or control surfaces.

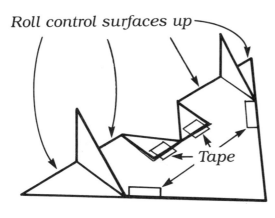

Illus. 148

Once you've bent up these rear control surfaces, slip a paper clip or two over *Cruiser's* nose, and it's ready for launching!

Launch it gently. Just give it a push into the air. Don't try to snap it or throw it. *Cruiser* likes to take things easy.

A good way to get *Cruiser* going is to grasp the middle of its trailing edge, with your thumb under the airplane, and your two fingers on top. Give the plane a little push into the air—don't try to launch it too hard.

The weight of the paper you used will determine your need for as many as three paper clips on the nose to trim this fabulous flier properly. Space the clips so that *Cruiser* does not have more paper clip weight on one side than it has on the other.

Although this airplane will step through the air, its glide path is long enough so that it is difficult to make out the little drops in elevation. If you wish, try bending or rolling the trailing edges of the two vertical stabilizers. Bend both stabilizers in the same direction.

Don't make drastic stabilizer changes, or your airplane will go into a spin and crash. You can always change the trim so that your *Cruiser* banks.

Dancer

First fold a sheet of notebook paper or typing paper in half the short way. Unfold the paper so that the middle fold makes a little mountain as it sticks up towards you. *Dancer* should look just like the drawing shown in Illus. 149.

The two dotted lines in Illus. 149 show where you'll fold *Dancer* next. Before you fold, take a quick look at Illus. 150 to see how your airplane will look with these folds in place.

Be sure the tips of the folded edges come right to the middle fold. Try to space the two other ends of the folds so they come out one inch from the middle fold at the airplane's nose. Check Illus. 150 to be sure you're on the right track.

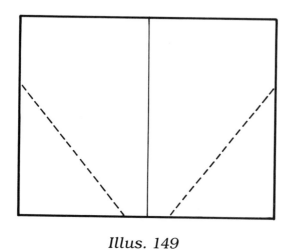

Illus. 149

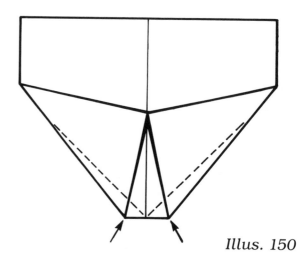

Illus. 150

The two dotted lines in Illus. 150 show where you'll make your next pair of folds. Make these folds so that the two corners indicated by the arrows meet right along *Dancer's* middle fold. *Dancer* now looks very much like the drawing seen in Illus. 151.

When you fold along the dotted line shown in Illus. 151, your airplane should match the one shown in Illus. 152.

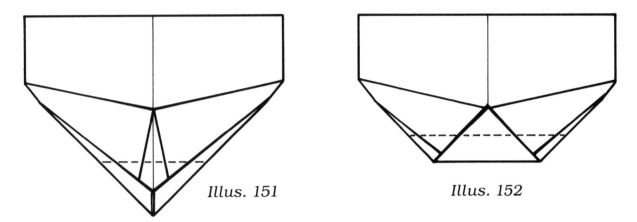

Illus. 151   Illus. 152

Space this fold so that the nose tip ends up right on top of the two corners you originally folded in to meet at the middle fold. Check Illus. 152 to see how things look with this fold finished.

Now fold along the dotted line shown in Illus. 152. Once that fold is in place and creased down firmly, *Dancer* is seen in Illus. 153.

Broadway, here we come!

Fold along the dotted line shown in Illus. 153 and you'll be almost done. Check the drawing shown in Illus. 154 to make sure your airplane matches the one shown. Fold the airplane along its middle fold, and

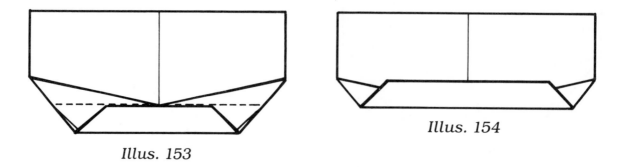

Illus. 153

Illus. 154

you'll be at the step shown in Illus. 155. Rotate your paper airplane as shown.

Fold down the wing nearer to you along the dotted line shown in Illus. 155. Turn the airplane over and fold down the second wing to match the first.

With the wings folded into place and still folded down, the airplane should look like Illus. 156.

Fold up the tip of the wing nearer you along the dotted line shown in Illus. 156. Turn the airplane over and fold up the other wing tip in exactly the same way.

Illus. 155

Illus. 156

Spread *Dancer's* wings so that it looks like the front view shown in Illus. 157. The two upright wing tips will act as vertical stabilizers.

Bend up the trailing edges of both wings between the fuselage and the stabilizers. Now test-fly your *Dancer*.

Launch it by just giving it a push into the air. It will do a fancy job of stepping through the air as it glides forward. *Dancer* will make a series of dips and fancy downward steps as it glides across the room.

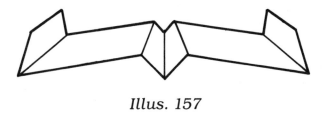

Illus. 157

Experiment with the trailing edges of the wings until *Dancer* takes exactly the proper steps to make it the sort of airplane any builder would be proud of.

Delta

The best way to describe *Delta* would be to call it a flying triangle. This flying triangle steps through the air and covers quite a bit of ground during its flight. Most people will take one look at *Delta* and will be absolutely certain it won't fly. You and *Delta* will prove them wrong.

Begin with a square piece of notebook paper or typing paper. Fold it diagonally and then crease the fold. Unfold the paper—you have what is shown in Illus.

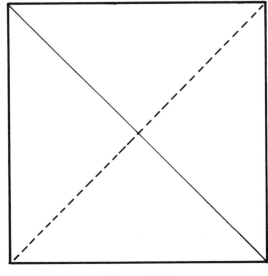

Illus. 158

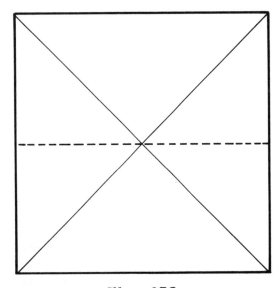

Illus. 159

158. The dotted line shows where to make your next diagonal fold.

Make the second diagonal fold, crease it, and then unfold the paper so that *Delta* looks like the drawing in Illus. 159. The dotted line shown in Illus. 159 shows where to fold next.

Make the middle fold and crease it. Unfold the paper, turn it over, and make the middle fold again. Folding the paper in the opposite direction will make this middle fold limber.

Now you've reached the point shown in Illus. 160. Push in on the two sides at the points shown by the two arrows in the drawing. As you've done for several other airplanes, push in the two sides towards each other, so that the paper forms the triangle you see in Illus. 161.

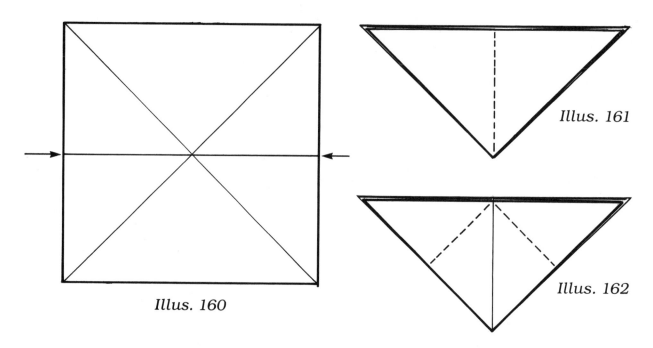

Illus. 160

Illus. 161

Illus. 162

The dotted line in Illus. 161 shows your next fold. Fold *Delta* in half and then unfold it again so it looks like Illus. 161—your airplane now has a middle fold.

From this point on, the folds involve only the top layer of *Delta*. This top layer is two sheets thick, but it acts as one layer because the fold holds together the two sheets of paper. Check the dotted lines shown in Illus. 162. They show your next folds.

When you make these folds, be sure that the edges of the paper come right to the middle fold you just made in the previous step.

Once this pair of folds is in place, *Delta* should look like the one shown in Illus. 163. The two dotted lines in Illus. 163 show the next pair of folds. Once again, make sure that when you fold the paper over, the edges should come right to *Delta's* middle fold. With this folding completed, you've reached Illus. 164.

Look at the dotted lines shown in Illus. 164. These are the final folds needed. They're also just a bit tricky, so be extra careful to do them properly.

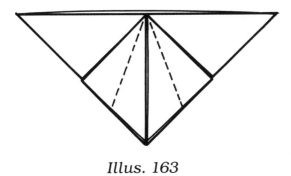

Illus. 163

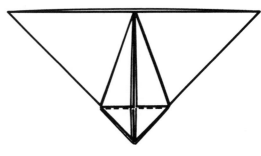

Illus. 164

Fold up the two points of paper along the dotted line. Crease the folds. Tuck those little triangular points of paper into the pocket of paper (between the top layer and the next layer you created when you made the last fold). Work these points you just folded in between these layers. Your airplane should look like the one shown in Illus. 165. Use two small pieces of tape to hold the paper flat, as shown in Illus. 165.

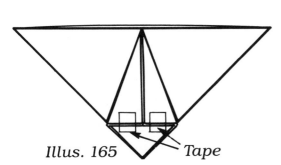

Illus. 165 Tape

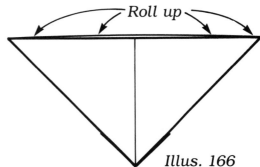

Roll up

Illus. 166

Roll up the trailing edges of *Delta's* wing a bit before its first test flight. The drawing in Illus. 166 shows that you'll roll up this trailing edge along the entire distance, from one wing tip to the other. Once the trailing edge of the wing is rolled or bent upward, *Delta* is ready for testing.

Launch this airplane a bit harder than you have been launching the other planes shown in this section. Tip *Delta's* nose up slightly and give it a good, solid push to send it into the air.

You'll probably have to add a paper clip to the nose for proper trim—but don't do that until you've first tested *Delta* without the clip.

When you get the trim just right, *Delta* will glide across the room, taking little downward steps with a nice glide between steps. Experiment with just how much to bend the trailing edges upward and how much to tip the nose skyward when you launch it.

Once you have things just right, surprise your friends with a flying triangle!

5.
Novelty Fliers

Novelty Fliers

After just building and flying aircraft such as a flying wing or a flying triangle, you might think you're an expert at making novelty paper airplanes. Let's get involved with some fabulous novelty fliers. They don't look at all like the paper airplanes you and your friends folded *before* you read this book.

Each of the novelty airplanes in this section has its own flight characteristics. Each looks quite a bit different from the airplanes you usually fold and fly. These novelty fliers will attract quite a bit of attention when you show them off.

Steady

Steady has a really different look. It will give you a nice, steady flight once you've finished with all the folding, cutting, and taping needed. Begin by folding a sheet of notebook paper (or other paper) in half lengthwise. Crease the fold, then unfold the paper so it looks like the drawing shown in Illus. 167.

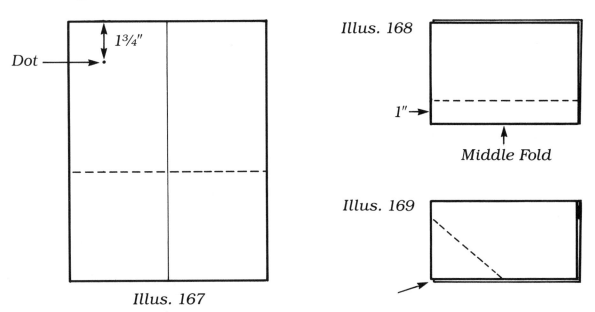

Illus. 168

Illus. 169

Illus. 167

The dotted line shown in Illus. 167 indicates your next fold. Don't make this fold yet. As you study the drawing, you'll see that this fold is not in the middle of the paper. When you make this fold the bottom edge of the paper should end up one and three-quarter inches below the top edge of the paper. Measure down one and three-quarter inches from the top of the paper, and make a dot to show that location. Fold up the bottom edge of the paper so that it comes right to that dot.

Fold the airplane back along its middle fold. Turn it so the middle fold is at the bottom, nearer you. It looks like the drawing in Illus. 168. Check the dotted line shown. This next fold is one inch from the middle fold.

Fold down the side nearer to you along the dotted line, and then crease the fold. Fold the opposite side so that it matches the first. After creasing the second side, your airplane should look like Illus. 169.

The dotted line shown in Illus. 169 indicates your next fold. When you make this fold, be certain that the corner of paper that the arrow points to in Illus. 169 comes right to the top of the fuselage. To be sure you have this fold in mind, check Illus. 170 to see how things look once the fold is made.

First fold the wing nearer to you. Use a small strip of cellophane tape or masking tape to hold this fold down. The tape is shown in Illus. 170. Once the first wing is folded and taped, do the same for the second wing.

Turn the airplane so its middle fold is towards you. This step appears as Illus. 171.

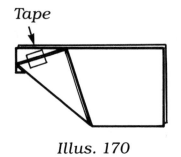

Illus. 170

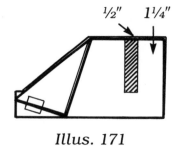

Illus. 171

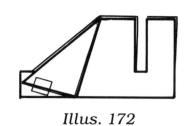

Illus. 172

Next, cut out the shaded area shown in Illus. 171. Be sure you don't cut any further than the top of the fuselage that you formed when you folded the wings down and into place. Make sure the section you cut out is exactly one-half inch wide. Make your first cut exactly one and three-quarter inches from the rear of the airplane.

This cut is where you originally made a dot and the folded the paper right to that dot. As you cut, your scissors will follow the edge of the extra layer of paper, but they won't cut it. If it helps, you could unfold *Steady* and make the first cut with the wings out flat. This makes it easier to follow the edge of the double layer of paper. Don't cut any further than the top edge of the fuselage. If you don't flatten the wings out, but cut through both wings at once, be sure to hold the paper firmly so it doesn't slip as you cut.

Make the second cut (the one closer to the tail) with the wings held firmly together. This cut is exactly one and one-quarter inches from the rear of the airplane. Illus. 171 shows this measurement.

Once you've made the two cuts, and then snipped off that half-inch of material (shaded in Illus. 171) you've arrived at Illus. 172.

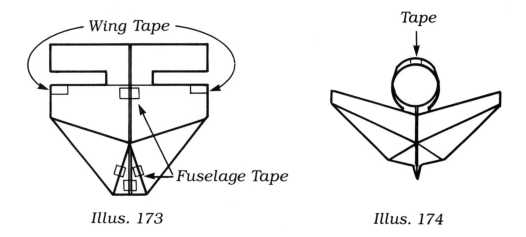

Illus. 173

Illus. 174

Now for a bit of taping. Check Illus. 173 (a top view of *Steady* with its wings outspread). Note that two pieces of tape hold the top of the fuselage so that both sides are pressed tightly together. Be sure to put the two little bits of tape on the trailing edges of the wings, as shown in the drawing.

Once this is done, deal with the tail section—it's now flopping around in the breeze. Pull the two sides of the tail section together so they form a circle. Illus.

174 shows a rear view of *Steady* with its tail formed properly.

Use a small piece of tape to hold together the two sides of the tail in the circle you just made.

The tail section is neither a vertical nor a horizontal stabilizer, since it's circular. It is still, however, a stabilizer and it helps to give *Steady* its name.

Before test-flying *Steady*, bend up or roll up the trailing edges of both wings slightly to improve its lift.

Slip a paper clip onto the airplane's nose and test-fly it. You may have to add several more paper clips in order to get *Steady* properly trimmed. Until you get just enough nose weight, this airplane tends to stall because of its peculiar tail construction.

Once you have the right combination of paper clips and wing trailing-edge bending, *Steady* will give you a nice, steady, flight. It's also a real eye-catcher because of its strange tail construction.

Darter

This cute little airplane is a real novelty flier. *Darter* is special because you launch it by blowing through a soda straw.

Cut a sheet of notebook paper or other paper in half—about five and one-half inches by eight and one-half inches. Use the very lightest paper you have. Keep the other half of the sheet of paper. You'll use it for *Darter's* launching tube.

Fold the half sheet of paper down the middle lengthwise and then unfold it. *Darter* should now look like Illus. 175.

The two dotted lines in Illus. 175 show where to make your next folds. Be sure to bring the edges of the paper you fold over right to the middle fold. Illus. 176

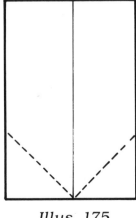

Illus. 175

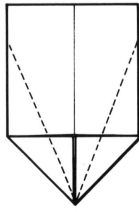

Illus. 176

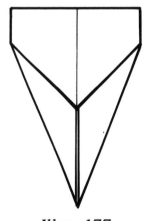

Illus. 177

shows the airplane after you make these two last folds. Check the two dotted lines to see where you'll be folding next. Make certain the edges of the paper come right to the middle of the airplane when you make this pair of folds. With these folds completed, *Darter* is seen in Illus. 177.

Now fold the airplane along its middle fold. It should look just like the drawing in Illus. 178. The dotted line in the drawing shows where you'll make your wing folds.

Fold down the wing nearer to you along the dotted line and then crease the fold well. Try to make this fold so it starts exactly at the nose point and ends about three-quarters inch higher at the airplane's tail. After folding the first wing, turn the airplane over and fold down the second wing to match the first.

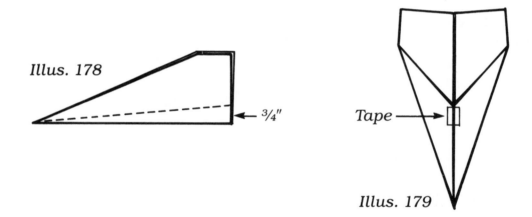

Illus. 178   ← 3/4"

Tape →

Illus. 179

Once both wings are folded, it's time for a small piece of tape. Illus. 179 shows a top view of *Darter* with the tape in place. When you press the tape onto the top of the airplane, lift both wings (just a bit) to give them some positive dihedral.

Now it's time to make use of the other half sheet of paper. You set this sheet aside just a minute or two ago.

Cut about three inches off the bottom of this half sheet of paper. You should have a piece of material five and one-half inches square. Now roll that piece of paper, forming a hollow tube five and one-half inches long. A good way to do this is to roll the paper around a pencil.

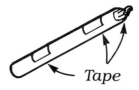

Before you start taping your tube so that it looks like Illus. 180, slip the pencil out and check the hollow middle, using your drinking straw. The tube needs to be large enough so that the straw can slip into and out of it easily. If your tube is too tight, just let the rolled paper loosen a bit. On the other hand, if the inside of the tube is larger than the straw, you can tighten up the roll of paper slightly.

Use two pieces of tape to keep the tube from unrolling, as shown in Illus. 180. Once the tube is taped, press one end of it together and use a third piece of tape to secure that end in an airtight seal. Check this seal by blowing gently into the tube. If you can feel any air escaping through the taped end, add another bit of tape. Your tube should be airtight so that none of the air escapes, as you blow through the straw.

Now attach the launching tube to the *Darter*. It might help if someone lends you an extra hand to help hold the airplane, the launching tube, and the tape.

Turn *Darter* over on a table or desk so its fuselage sticks up into the air. Cut off a three-inch long strip of tape. Press the middle of the tape onto the tube about one and one-half inches from the crimped and taped end.

Hold the tube right over the fuselage so that the crimped end of the tube and the airplane's nose point are both lined up, as seen in Illus. 181.

Illus. 181

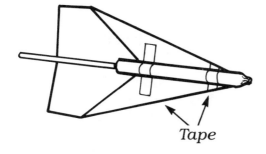

Tape

Let the launching tube rest on the fuselage. Press the tape around the tube, and onto the fuselage. The ends of the tape will extend onto the bottoms of the wings. If there's extra tape, fold it over the wing so that it ends up on top.

Once you have the first piece of tape in place, repeat the process and tape the rear of the launching tube in place. Just apply the tape about one and one-half inches from the open end of the tube, and then tape the tube onto the airplane a second time.

Don't crush the launching tube while you're doing this taping. The tube has to remain round—the drinking straw must slip in and out easily.

Launch *Darter* by pushing a soda straw into the launching tube. Hold the straw with one hand and steady the airplane with your other hand. Breathe one sharp, hard blow into the straw. Let go of the airplane when you blow! *Darter* will take off with its "jet-assisted" takeoff and it will then do a nice glide for you. Bend up the trailing edges of the airplane's wings to give it a bit of added lift. This will compensate for the weight of the launching tube.

Now that you know how to make a soda-straw launcher, you may want to experiment with some of the earlier airplanes you've already made. Use the lightest paper available when making airplanes you'll launch in this manner.

Make airplanes out of smaller paper than you used the first time. Make the launching tube shorter and lighter to improve flight characteristics of some of your experimental models.

Diamond

As soon as you fold this airplane's wings, you'll see the reason for its name.

Fold a sheet of notebook paper or typing paper in half the short way, giving you a folded sheet of paper looking just like the one shown in Illus. 182.

The dotted line in Illus. 182 shows where to make your first wing fold. This fold should be three-quarters inch above the middle fold. Fold down the wing nearer to you, then turn the paper over and fold the other wing down to match the first.

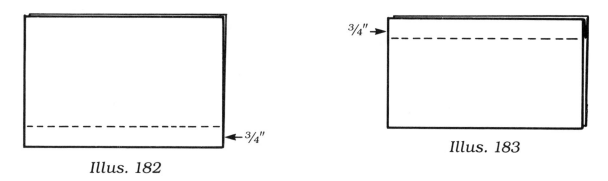

Illus. 182

Illus. 183

The dotted line in Illus. 183 indicates your next fold. It's exactly in line with the middle fold you made first.

Fold up one wing along the dotted line. This fold should exactly match the middle fold already in place. Do the same with the second wing. Now you've reached Illus. 184.

With your scissors, cut out the shaded area shown in Illus. 184. This shaded area is two inches high by two and one-half inches wide.

Measure the area to be cut and mark it on the wing nearer to you. Hold the two wings together so you cut them both at the same time. Don't let the two pieces of paper slip or slide as you cut. You might end up with an airplane with one side different from the other.

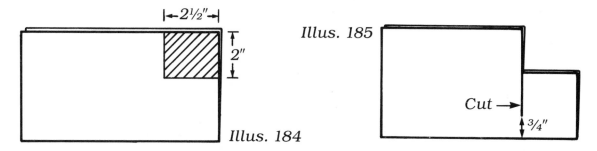

Illus. 185

Illus. 184

Illus. 185 shows the airplane after this cutting is done. Now make the cut line shown in this drawing. Hold both sides of the airplane together and make one cut do the job for both sides. Don't cut into the fuselage! Stop cutting before you cut into the four layers of folded material inside.

Turn the airplane over on the desk or table so that the fuselage sticks up into the air, and the wings and tail

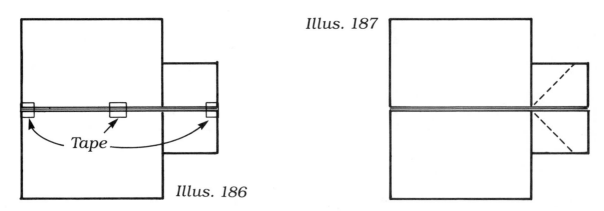

Illus. 187

Illus. 186

Tape

section are now flat on the tabletop. Illus. 186 shows the airplane in this position.

Press the four layers of the fuselage tightly together and use three pieces of tape to hold the fuselage so it doesn't unfold. Illus. 186 shows where this tape goes. Put the tape over the *front* of the fuselage and over the *rear* (at the tail) rather than on the underside of the fuselage, where the middle piece of tape is positioned.

Now it's time to do some more folding. Leave *Diamond* flat on its top, just the way it is. Illus. 187 shows

Don't cut through the fuselage!

Never mind the fuselage, look at my tie!

the tail folds. The edge of the paper of each fold should come right up to the fuselage.

Use small pieces of cellophane tape or masking tape to fasten these tail folds down tightly. Illus. 188 shows the tape already in place. The dotted lines in Illus. 188 show your next folds. When you fold the wings along these folds, the edges of the wings will end up about one-quarter inch away from the fuselage.

The drawing in Illus. 189 shows the first wing folds in place. Use two small pieces of tape to hold these wing folds in place.

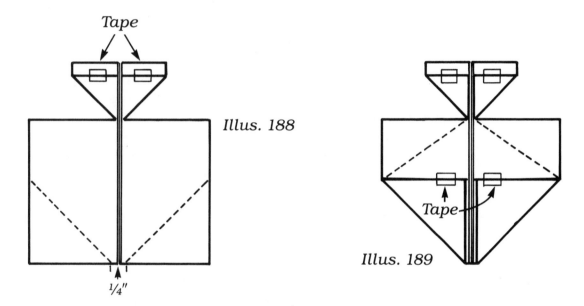

Illus. 188

Illus. 189

The final folds are shown as dotted lines in Illus. 189. Make each fold and crease it. The fold will extend over the front part of the wing. After creasing these folds, tuck these two corners under the front part of the wing. The front of the wing will hold the rear part in place. Illus. 190 shows the airplane with these folds made and the corners tucked under and into place.

Turn *Diamond* over. Use a small piece of tape to make the wings lift slightly. The tape is shown in Illus. 191. Try to give the wings enough dihedral so that the tips of the wings are about one-half inch higher than where the wing meets the fuselage.

Slip a paper clip onto *Diamond's* nose and give it a test flight. You'll probably find that it helps *Diamond's*

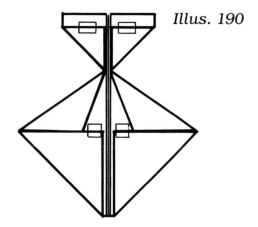

Illus. 190

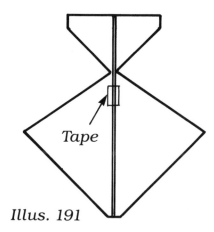

Tape

Illus. 191

trim to roll or bend up the trailing edges of its horizontal stabilizer slightly. Add another paper clip if *Diamond* seems to want to stall during flight. This airplane gives good long flights—it's also an excellent airplane for distance.

Diamond has another flight characteristic you'll see if you watch the airplane carefully. Its wings will rise during flight, then drop back down into place as it slows for a landing. At least my airplane's wings did.

Triad

Triad means three. Several things about your *Triad* have three as an important number.

Once again you'll need a sheet of notebook paper or typing paper. You'll also need some file cards or some very stiff paper.

Let's begin with *Triad's* fuselage. Turn the paper so that the long side faces you, as shown in Illus. 192. Fold over the side nearer to you about five-eighths inch. A slightly bigger fold of three-quarters inch won't cause any problems.

Illus. 192 shows that first fold. The dotted lines, of course, indicate the rest of the folds to be made. Just fold the paper over and over until it is all used up.

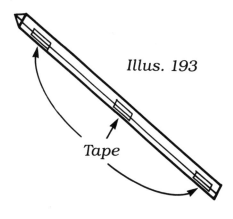

Illus. 193

5/8"

Illus. 192

Don't tape the loose edge yet. Unfold the paper until you reach the first fold. Turn the fuselage into a hollow triangular "tube." Form the base and the two sides of the triangle with three sections of the folded paper. Overlap the folded paper around the hollow triangle. Be sure to maintain the fuselage's triangular shape.

Once the paper is all wrapped onto the triangular fuselage, as seen in Illus. 193, use two or three strips of tape to keep the whole thing from unfolding.

Now draw *Triad's* front and rear fins. Make *three* of each, using the file cards. Begin with the smaller front fins. These fins combine wing and stabilizer into one.

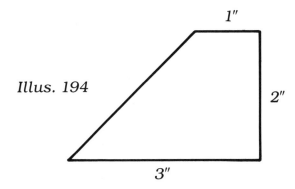

1"

Illus. 194

2"

3"

Illus. 194 shows that the base of this fin is three inches long. Draw that line first, on the stiff material you're using for the fins, unless you feel better making a separate pattern. Now draw the two-inch trailing edge from the base upwards. Next draw the one-inch top edge from the trailing edge forwards.

Finally, connect the leading edge of the base line and the top line with a slanting line. This line is about two and three-quarter inches long. When you connect the two leading edges of the lines (as directed), the fin outline is finished.

Triad needs three of these front fins. If you use regular paper, try folding a sheet into thirds so you cut all three fins at once. When you cut three layers at once, don't let the bottom layers of paper slip, or you'll end up with bad-looking fins.

Unless your scissors are very sharp and you are very skillful, it's probably not a good idea to cut three file cards at once. Use a fin you already cut out as a quick pattern ("template") for the following fins.

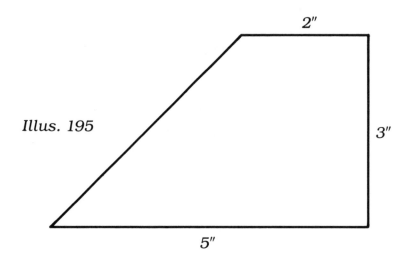

Illus. 195

The rear fin is slightly larger than the front fins but it's exactly the same shape. Illus. 195 shows that its base is five inches long. The trailing edge is three inches high and the top is two inches long. The slanting edge (it's also the leading edge) is approximately four and one-quarter inches long.

Once you've cut out the three front fins and the three rear fins, it's time to assemble *Triad*.

Place one front fin so that its leading point is right at the nose of the fuselage. Line up the base of the fin so it matches the fold in the fuselage. Tape it on both its

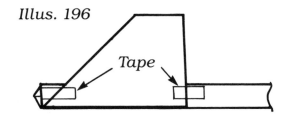

Illus. 196

Tape

leading edge and on its trailing edge; Illus. 196 shows how.

Once the first front fin is in place, attach one rear fin. Illus. 197 shows that this fin's trailing edge is even with the airplane's tail; its base also lines up exactly with the fuselage fold.

Taping the leading edge of the rear fin is no problem. However, when you tape the trailing edge, press half the length of your tape strip onto the fin. Fold the other half into the hollow middle of the fuselage and press the tape firmly into place.

Now that you know how to attach the fins to the fuselage, tape the four others into place. Lay the airplane on your table or desk so that the fins already in place are flat on the top of the table or desk. Tape the next pair of fins into place just as you did the first pair. Check Illus. 197 to see how the airplane looks as you're doing this. Note that this drawing shows before *and* after.

Turn *Triad* again and tape the final pair of fins into place. Don't worry if the fins already in place seem to bend a bit when they touch the top of the table or desk. Just don't push down on the fuselage—the fins will come through the procedure just fine.

Once all six fins are in place, *Triad* is ready for its first test flight. Illus. 197 shows two views of *Triad* with all its fins in place.

With all the weight of the large tail section, expect *Triad* to be out of balance. One or two paper clips will be needed on *Triad's* nose to get it properly trimmed. Be sure to put both clips (if you use two) on the same side of the triangular fuselage.

When you launch *Triad*, do so with the paper clip (or clips) on the lower side of the fuselage. If you want to

Illus. 197 shows three views of the fins attached to the hollow triangular body. The view on the upper right is schematic.

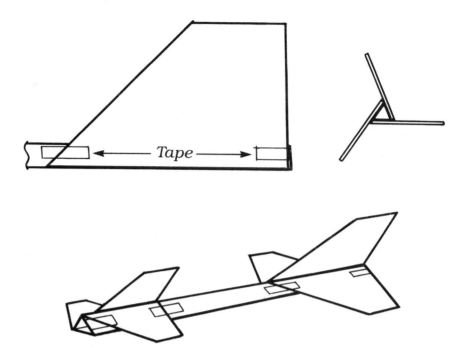

see why this is so, launch your airplane with the clips on one side or the other. It won't hurt *Triad*, but its flight path may seem strange.

If your *Triad* behaves anything like mine, it will fly a short distance before making one single twist or a mid-air roll. After this, it will finish its flight. Who knows how your *Triad* will act? It might even give you *two* twists or rolls, though that may be expecting too much.

After you've flown *Triad* a few times, you may decide to make a few changes in a new model. Make the fuselage folds closer together so that the new fuselage isn't as wide as the first.

You may even want to change the size (or even the basic shape) of the fins. Feel free to try this. Sometimes experimentation produces a better paper airplane. At other times changes won't work out. To find out how changes will affect an airplane's flight, make the changes and begin test flights.

Wonder

This fabulous paper airplane is named *Wonder*—you'll wonder whether it will fly once it is finished. Wonder no more. It will fly perfectly—although it *does* look slightly different from the airplanes you've been making so far.

You'll need two sheets of notebook paper or typing paper for *Wonder*. Begin with *Wonder's* fuselage. This fuselage is completely different from that of any of your previous fabulous paper airplanes. Fold a sheet of paper lengthwise so that it looks like the one shown in Illus. 198.

The dotted line shown in Illus. 198 shows your next fold. This new fold will become the middle fold of the fuselage.

After making the middle fold (as shown in Illus. 198), you're at the point shown by the drawing in Illus. 199. You'll need your scissors for just a minute.

Cut out the two shaded areas shown in the drawing. Each of these cuts ends one-half inch from the middle fold. Don't cut any closer to the fold. Each cut is one-quarter inch wide at the top.

Note the measurements shown in Illus. 199 before you begin cutting. Measure two inches down from the end of the folded paper. This is the first cut to make. Hold the folded paper together so that you cut both sides of the airplane at the same time. Cut at an angle. Stop cutting one-half inch from the middle fold.

Move your scissors over one-quarter inch and cut down at an angle so you meet the end of your first cut. The shaded section (seen in the drawing) will be removed.

Now cut away the rear section. Start your cut one-quarter inch from the end of the paper. Remember to angle the cut so that it ends one-half inch from the fold. When you finish cutting, flatten the airplane's middle fold so that the two layers of paper lie flat on your desk or table. Illus. 200 shows how *Wonder* looks once the cutting is done and the middle fold is flattened out.

Fold in both sides along the dotted lines shown in Illus. 200. Make sure both edges meet exactly at the middle fold.

Illus. 201 shows these folds already in place. Tape down the folded paper as shown. Fold in both sides along the dotted lines shown in Illus. 201. These folds

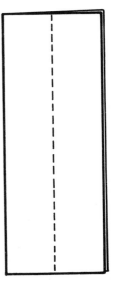

Illus. 198

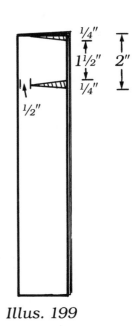

Illus. 199

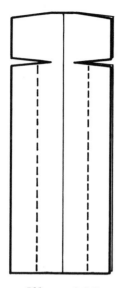

Illus. 200

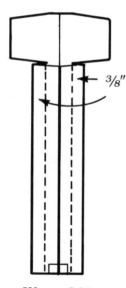

3/8"

Illus. 201

Illus. 202

are **not** exactly halfway between the middle fold and the outside edges of the paper. Make these folds about three-eighths inch wide. When the folds are finished, let these sides stand straight up so that the fuselage looks like a flattened-out "U" if you look at it from the front end. Illus. 202 shows a front-end view of the "U" shape.

The dotted line in the next drawing (Illus. 203) shows where to make your next fold. Fold this section in half along the dotted line to form a horizontal stabilizer.

Illus. 204 shows you three pieces of tape on the horizontal stabilizer. Two small bits of tape are near the tips of the stabilizer. A larger piece of tape fastens down the middle of the stabilizer and also holds the fuselage folds in place.

Now turn the fuselage over so it looks like the drawing in Illus. 205. Fold up the tips of the horizontal stabilizer along the dotted lines. Now you can set aside the fuselage for a minute or two.

Fold the second sheet of paper in half the long way. Unfold it so that it looks like Illus. 206.

The dotted line in Illus. 206 shows where to make your next fold. Just fold the paper in half and then unfold it again so that it lies flat.

Now check Illus. 207. The two dotted lines are your next folds. In order to get these folds in the right places, we need to do a little measuring. Measure along the top of the paper two and one-half inches to the left of the middle line. Mark that point with a dot. Then measure two and one-half inches to the right of the middle line and mark that location with another dot.

Move your ruler to the lower edge of the paper. Measure two and one-half inches both to the right and to the left of the middle fold. Mark both points with dots.

Now look back at Illus. 207 one more time to be sure you have your dots in the proper locations.

In order to make folding easier, draw a line from the dot at the upper left of the page to the dot at the lower right. You're just drawing one of the fold lines seen in Illus. 207. Push down on your ballpoint pen (or your

Who writes your material, birdbeak?

Hey . . . that fuselage looks like "U"!

pencil) firmly. This will score the paper and make it easier to fold. Fold along the line you just drew. Crease the fold, then unfold it.

Now connect the dot at the upper right with the dot at the lower left. Remember to push down firmly on your ballpoint pen or your pencil. Fold along this line. Crease the fold, then unfold the paper once again.

Just to make the next step easier, let's do a few more quick folds. Fold the diagonal fold you just made *backwards* and then crease it.

Unfold the paper and then reverse and crease the other diagonal fold in the same way. Once you've done

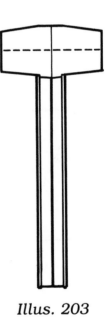

Illus. 203

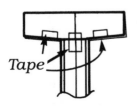

Tape

Illus. 204

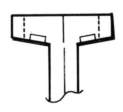

Illus. 205

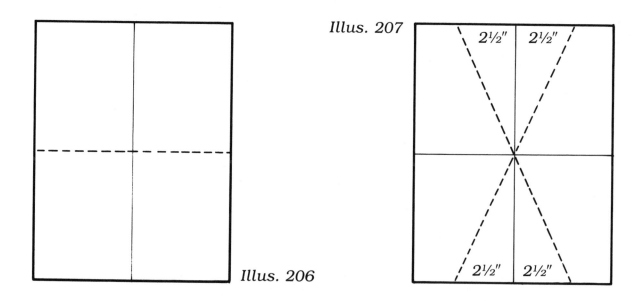

Illus. 207

Illus. 206

this, fold the middle fold backwards as well. That's the middle fold which runs between the two diagonal folds you've just made.

With all this folding and refolding done, we're now at Illus. 208. Do a bit of pushing so that the sheet of paper turns into the airplane wing shown in Illus. 209.

Push the sides of the paper towards one another at the points shown by the single arrows in Illus. 208.

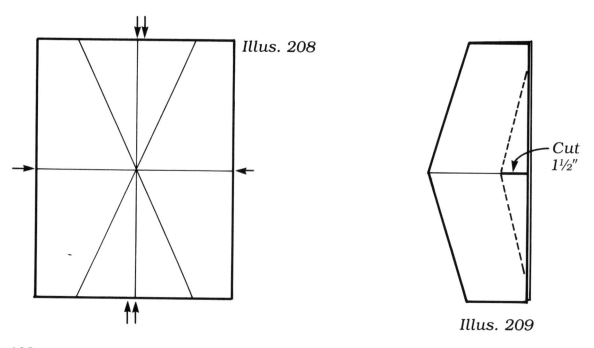

Illus. 208

Cut
1½"

Illus. 209

The middle line (indicated by the double arrows) will just fold up inside the paper and vanish from view. What you'll have left is shown in Illus. 209.

Make the cut shown in Illus. 209 right along the wing's middle fold. This cut should be one and one-half inches long.

Once the cut is made, fold down the trailing edges of the wing along the two dotted lines shown in Illus. 209. After folding down the trailing edges, turn the wing over so that it looks like the one shown in Illus. 210.

There are six pieces of tape shown in Illus. 210. Two bits of tape will hold each fold tightly against the rest of the wing. You could glue these flaps of paper down instead of taping them.

Two other pieces of tape are used on the wing's leading edge. Each piece of tape wraps around the front of the wing to hold together both layers of wing.

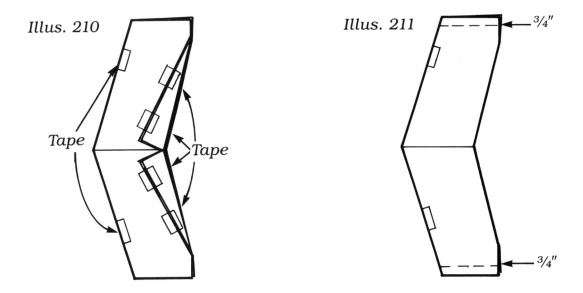

Illus. 210

Tape

Tape

Illus. 211

³/₄″

³/₄″

After all this tape is in place, turn the wing back over. Illus. 211 shows the top of the wing. The dotted lines show where to fold up only the top layer of paper near each wing tip. There are *two* layers of paper at the wing tips—you'll fold up only the top layer. Make each fold about three-quarters inch from the tip of the wing.

Now to assemble *Wonder*. Illus. 212 shows the wing in place. The artist didn't draw it backwards—that's just the way *Wonder* looks. The stabilizer is at the airplane's nose and its wing is at the rear of the fuselage. And, *yes*, it will fly perfectly!

Tape the leading edge of the wing onto the top of the fuselage, as shown in the drawing. Then tape down the trailing edge by placing one end of the tape on the wing and folding the other end of the tape over the end of the fuselage and then pressing the tape tightly against the bottom side of the fuselage. This is inside the "U" shape.

Launch *Wonder* by taking hold of its fuselage and giving it an easy throw. The horizontal stabilizer leads the way and the wing follows at the rear.

The vertical tips of the stabilizer and the wing all act as vertical stabilizers and help give *Wonder* a straight, even glide.

You'll probably need to slip a paper clip over the airplane's nose—and bend up the trailing edges of the wing to give the airplane slightly more lift. When you have *Wonder* trimmed correctly, it will be good for long, steady flights.

When you hold up your fabulous paper airplane in (what looks like) a backwards position and then proceed to demonstrate a long, perfect glide, you'll be the *wonder* of the neighborhood.

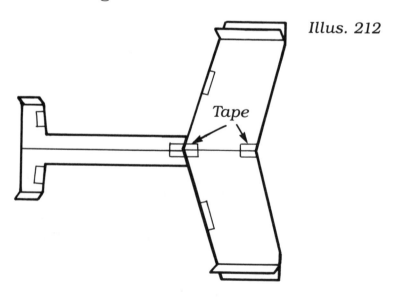

Illus. 212

Tape

6.
Soda-Straw Fliers

Soda-Straw Fliers

The fabulous paper airplanes we'll build in this section all use soda straws for their fuselages. They *look* strange, but you'll stop thinking about how different these *Soda-Straw Fliers* look once you launch them into the air. One of these *Soda-Straw Fliers* uses a catapult-assisted takeoff that sends it into flight at super speed.

Gull

If you've even seen a gull in flight, you know how its wings move. When you finish this paper airplane, its wings will resemble those of a flying gull.

Begin with a piece of notebook paper or typing paper six inches wide and about eleven inches long. Fold this piece of paper in half the long way, giving you the three-inch by eleven-inch sheet shown in Illus. 213. If you use a standard-size sheet of paper, save the two-and-one-half-inch by eleven-inch scrap. You'll use this scrap piece later, for the tail.

Fold the paper in the middle along the dotted line shown in Illus. 213. Unfold the paper so that it looks

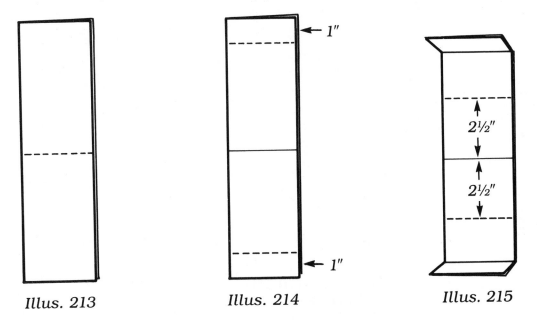

Illus. 213   Illus. 214   Illus. 215

like the drawing shown in Illus. 214. The fold should look like a little valley in the middle of the paper.

Fold up the tips of both wings towards you, along the dotted lines shown in Illus. 214. These two folds should both be one inch from the ends of the paper.

The *Gull* wing is now seen in Illus. 215. The pair of dotted lines shown in this drawing are your next two folds. Measure two and one-half inches from the middle fold and make these two next folds at that point. Make two dots two and one-half inches from the middle, so that these two folds are exactly the same distance from the middle. Fold the ends of the wings *away* from you. These two folds will look like little ridges between the valleys formed by the middle fold and the folds at the wing tips.

Lay your drinking straw into the middle fold so that one inch of the straw sticks out towards the front of the

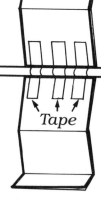

Illus. 216

paper, as shown in Illus. 216. The *folded* side of the wing is the leading edge. If you use the open side, your wing will try to open in flight and your *Gull* will crash.

Use three strips of tape to attach the wing to the soda-straw fuselage. Center the tape over the straw. Press the tape onto the middle of the straw. Work the tape down around the straw without letting the ends of the tape touch the wing. Attach the tape firmly to the straw before taping onto the wing. Finish taping by pressing the tape onto the top of the wing. Three strips will hold the wing in place.

Now for the tail section. The leftover strip of paper you had when you cut out the wing is just fine for the

Illus. 217

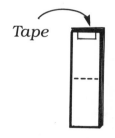

Illus. 218

Illus. 219

tail. This strip should be eight inches long by two and one-half inches wide.

Fold this strip in half lengthwise so that you have a narrow strip of paper eight inches long, one and one-quarter inches wide, and two layers thick. Illus. 217 shows this strip. The dotted line shows your next fold.

Fold the paper in half along the dotted line shown in Illus. 217. Tape the loose ends together by folding a short piece of tape over them.

Illus. 218 shows this tape in place. A dotted line shows your next fold.

Fold the tail section in half and then unfold it so it looks like the drawing shown in Illus. 219. Be sure this fold looks like a little valley when the tail is flat on the desk or the table in front of you.

Fold up both tips along the dotted lines shown in Illus. 219. Crease these folds sharply so that the tips stand straight up to form vertical stabilizers.

Place the tail of the (straw) fuselage over the middle fold of the stabilizer you just made. Use two strips of tape to attach the fuselage to the stabilizer. Just as you did with the wing, make sure that the tape is fastened firmly to as much of the straw as possible. Illus. 220 shows *Gull* almost ready for flight.

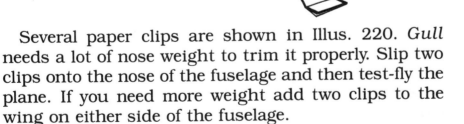

Illus. 220

Several paper clips are shown in Illus. 220. *Gull* needs a lot of nose weight to trim it properly. Slip two clips onto the nose of the fuselage and then test-fly the plane. If you need more weight add two clips to the wing on either side of the fuselage.

Experiment with bending up the wing's trailing edges. This will give the right amount of lift to trim the airplane. If you want, make pairs of cuts one-quarter inch deep on the wing's trailing edge to make control flaps or ailerons you can bend at an angle.

Once *Gull* is trimmed correctly, it will fly nicely. Its wings will move upwards during flight.

If you wish, make another *Gull* using lightweight cardboard, such as file folders. If you use cardboard, make the wing and the tail section only one layer thick. Heavier material is just too much for *Gull*.

Smooth Sailer

Your second soda-straw flier, a smooth-gliding airplane, does a fabulous job of reacting to air currents.

For *Smooth Sailer* you'll need two drinking straws. Using scissors, make a cut down one side of one of the straws as shown in Illus. 221. This cut should be one and one-half inches long. Make the cut on just one side of the straw.

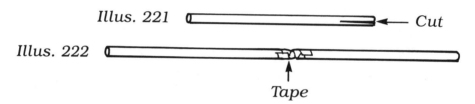

Illus. 221 — *Cut*

Illus. 222

Tape

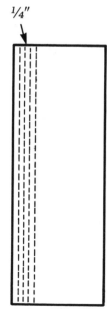

¼"

Illus. 223

Press slightly on both sides of the cut straw. Because of the cut you made, the sides will roll around each other, forming a little cone at the end of the straw. Push this little cone into one end of the *other* straw, so that the two straws look like the drawing shown in Illus. 222.

Wrap a piece of tape around the joint. Make sure that the tape sticks to both straws. You don't want *Smooth Sailer* coming apart in flight.

Cut a sheet of notebook paper or typing paper four inches wide and as long as the sheet of paper (usually about eleven inches). This will be *Smooth Sailer's* wing.

Check the dotted lines shown in Illus. 223. These fold lines are one-quarter inch apart. Make the first fold one-quarter inch from the edge of the wing; now crease it carefully.

*Don't cut yourself,
with those scissors,
buddy!*

Roll that double layer of paper over to make the next fold. Again, crease it well. Make the third and fourth folds in the same way. Be sure to crease these folds down firmly.

Illus. 224 shows the wing after these folds are all made. The side shown will become the bottom of the wing.

Use three short pieces of tape to hold the folded layers in place; Illus. 224 shows where to place the tape.

Turn the wing over so that the folded part faces down. Pull the wing tips together and bend (don't fold)

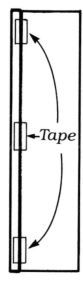

Illus. 224

the wing right in the middle. This will give you the wing's middle point. Place the wing on top of the drinking-straw fuselage as shown in Illus. 225. Be sure that the folded part of the wing is now at the wing's leading edge.

Leave four and one-half inches of soda straw between the tip of the fuselage and the leading edge of the wing.

Tape the wing to the fuselage using masking tape; this tape is tough. A short strip of tough fibre (filament) mailing tape will work, as well.

Illus. 226 shows where to make two scissor cuts in the tape before applying the tape to the wing and to the fuselage.

Place the uncut end of the tape on the top of the leading edge of the wing. Press it into place. Press the center of the cut end onto the top of the fuselage and then push it down firmly.

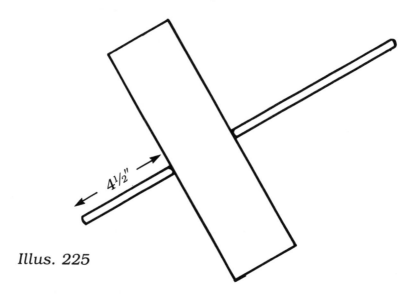

Illus. 225

Finally, bend the two sides of the cut section down and onto the sides of the fuselage. Once this is done, the leading edge of the wing should be firmly attached to the fuselage. The second drawing in Illus. 226 shows how to do this.

If you have only cellophane tape, don't try to make two cuts in the end of it. It tears too easily to hold up under much bending and twisting. Instead, make one cut down the middle of the cellophane tape. Then one

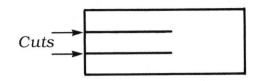

Cuts

Illus. 226 shows two views of the strip of tape used to connect the straw to the fuselage.

half will fasten to the top of the fuselage and the other half will fit down the side of the straw.

After getting one strip of either type of tape in place, repeat the process with a second strip. One cut section will go on top of the fuselage and the other cut section fastens down the side you didn't tape with the first strip.

Remember how to apply tape to soda-straw fuselages. You'll use this same method a number of times in this section.

Here's the time you can use an extra hand if one's available. Tape the trailing edge of the wing to the fuselage and put a bit of curve or *camber* into the wing.

Prepare your tape just the way you did the tape for the leading edge of the wing. Press the uncut end onto the wing's trailing edge.

Before attaching the tape to the fuselage, push the trailing edge *forward* so that the entire wing curves upwards. Illus. 227 shows a partial side view of the wing's end with this camber in place.

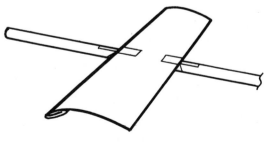

Illus. 227

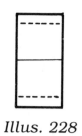

Illus. 228

Once the camber is in the wing, fasten the cut end of the tape to the fuselage. The hardest part in building *Smooth Sailer* is now behind you.

A piece of file card makes a perfect stabilizer for this airplane. Cut a piece of file card or other very lightweight cardboard four inches long by two inches wide.

Bring the two ends together to locate the middle of the card. Bend the card slightly along the middle, but don't crease it. Fold both ends of the card upwards along the dotted lines, as shown in Illus. 228. Crease these folds so that the ends of the card form a pair of vertical stabilizers.

Attach the stabilizer section to the fuselage so that the trailing edge of the stabilizer is exactly even with the rear of the fuselage. Use the same tape-cutting method you used when attaching the wing. Don't put any camber in the stabilizer.

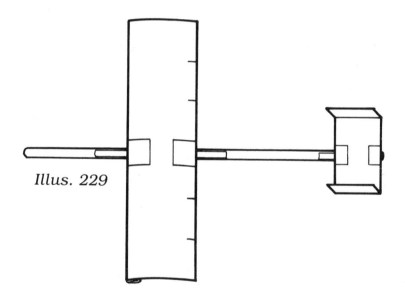

Illus. 229

Illus. 229 is a top view of the airplane. Note the two pairs of cuts in the wing's trailing edge. You may want to make these cuts so that you can bend control flaps, or you may prefer to bend up or roll up the wing's trailing edge. Either way will work just fine.

You'll probably need a paper clip for nose weight, but test *Smooth Sailer* first. If you do need a clip, just slip it onto the bottom side of the fuselage.

Give the wing a bit of dihedral angle to give this fabulous paper airplane a boost. Try it and see. The same is true of the horizontal stabilizer.

Be gentle with *Smooth Sailer* and work to get it properly trimmed. Once you have just the right combination of control flaps and a slight dihedral, you'll find that this airplane responds to air currents and that it does a fine flying job.

Stranger

The *Stranger* may not be the strangest flying airplane you'll ever see, but it certainly is stranger than most. Join two drinking straws together to form one long, skinny fuselage, exactly as you did for *Smooth Sailer*. Make a cut one and one-half inches long in one end of a straw and form that end into a little cone. Illus. 230 shows the cut already made, and the little cone already formed.

Push this cone into the open end of the other straw. Then wrap a strip of tape around the connection, making sure that the tape attaches to both straws, as seen in Illus. 231.

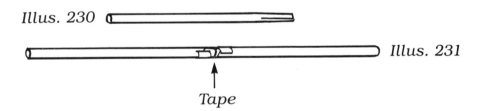

Illus. 230

Illus. 231

Tape

Now cut three strips of material from one sheet of notebook paper. The first strip should be one and one-quarter inches wide and six and one-half inches long.

Cut the second strip one inch wide and six inches long. Cut the third strip one and one-quarter inches wide by eight and one-half inches long.

Now form each strip into a loop (or a circle) of paper. Pull the narrow ends of each strip together; join these

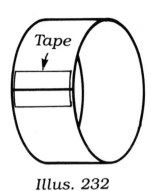

Illus. 232

two ends together using a strip of tape. Illus. 232 indicates how each of the strips will now look.

Now it's time to construct *Stranger*. If you have masking tape available, it's tougher than cellophane tape, and it works perfectly. Cut the ends of a piece of masking tape so that the tape fits easily around the drinking straw. Illus. 233 shows those three cuts in the end of the tape. The second drawing in Illus. 233 shows you how to fold down the outer edges of the cut tape and fold them onto the fuselage. If you're using cellophane tape, make just one cut in the center of the tape strip and then use two strips of the cellophane tape instead of just one strip of masking tape.

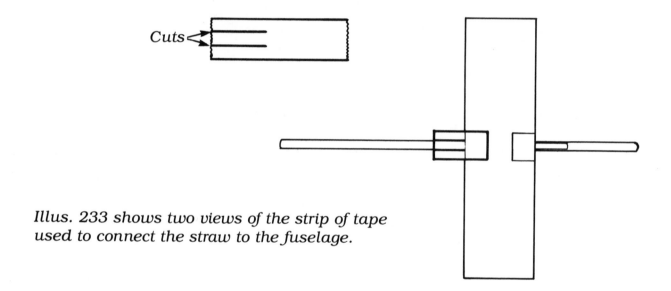

Illus. 233 shows two views of the strip of tape used to connect the straw to the fuselage.

Illus. 234

Begin with the first loop (the paper strip one and one-quarter by six and one-half inches). Tape the loop onto the end of the fuselage as shown in Illus. 234. The front of the loop should be even with the end of the fuselage.

Tape the front of the loop firmly onto the fuselage using one strip of tape. Then tape down the rear of the loop just as firmly, and the first loop is finished.

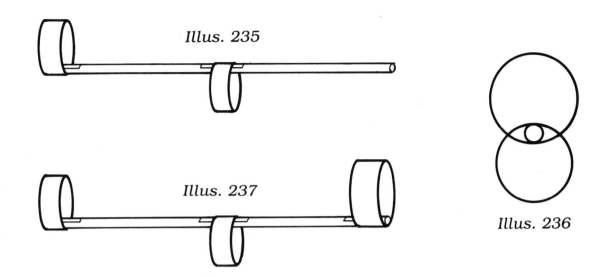

Illus. 235

Illus. 237

Illus. 236

Move on to the smallest of the three paper loops. Tape this loop onto the fuselage so it looks like the drawing shown in Illus. 235. Tape this small loop of paper halfway from the front to the rear of the fuselage.

This second paper loop must hang straight down from the fuselage and the first loop must stand straight up. In order for *Stranger* to fly properly these loops must be in a straight line with each other. Illus. 236 shows an end view of *Stranger* at this stage. Make sure you see how these loops have to line up.

Tape the second loop onto the fuselage with a strip of tape at the front of the loop and another at the rear of the loop. If you use cellophane tape, you'll probably use two strips of tape at the front and two more strips at the back.

To finish *Stranger*, tape the third and largest loop onto the rear of the fuselage. Illus. 237 shows all three loops in place.

Use two strips of tape on the final loop and make absolutely certain that this loop lines up exactly with the first loop. Be sure that these two loops are taped onto the soda-straw fuselage so that they both stand straight up from the fuselage.

To launch *Stranger*, just grasp it near the rear (where the largest loop is) of the fuselage and give it a quick forward thrust. Or, place your index finger at the rear of the fuselage as your thumb and other fingers grip the fuselage. Give your hand and forearm a little snap, and *Stranger* is off and flying.

If it stalls, add a paper clip to its nose. Slip the clip into the fuselage nose so that the clip fits over the lower side of the straw.

Stranger is designed to give you a long, steady flight. Don't be surprised if *Stranger* does a quick roll during flight, however. Some of these strange airplanes roll and some don't.

This soda-straw sailer will give your friends a real thrill. Although this airplane looks as though it can't fly at all, *Stranger* does a fabulous job in the air.

Dizzy

Dizzy is a catapult-assisted flier. It's fast and it flies high. You'd be better off flying *Dizzy* outdoors.

Begin with just one soda straw. *Dizzy* is a short little airplane. To make *Dizzy's* wing and tail section, use two small file cards. Or, just use one large file card. If you don't have file cards available, use a file folder or the very lightest similar material you can find.

Fold a file card in half so that it looks like the drawing shown in Illus. 238. Be sure the fold is at the bottom of the drawing. Now draw half the wing as shown in Illus. 238. For your first model, make the wing two and one-half inches front to back and four inches from tip to tip.

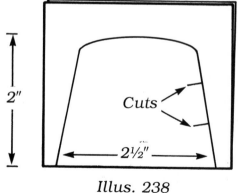

Illus. 238

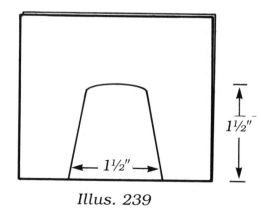

Illus. 239

Help! I'm not ready for a space launch!

Draw your "half wing" so it is two inches from the fold to the tip. Don't worry if your wing does not look exactly like Illus. 238. Just approximate the drawing.

Cut out the wing with the file card still folded so that both sides of the wing are identical. Make the cuts for the control flaps while the wing is still folded. These cuts should be one-fourth to three-eighths inch long.

Set aside the wing and now deal with the tail. Fold a new file card so you have to draw only half of the horizontal stabilizer.

Make the horizontal stabilizer one and one-half inches from leading edge to trailing edge and three inches tip-to-tip. The half you draw will be one and one-half inches from fold to tip. Illus. 239 shows how your stabilizer should look once you draw it on the folded file card. Cut out the stabilizer from the folded card. When you unfold the finished tail section, both sides should be exactly the same.

Now attach the wing and the stabilizer to the fuselage. *Dizzy's* fuselage fits under its wing and its tail, so you'll work with the wing and the tail on the table and the fuselage on top of both.

Dizzy's wing and its stabilizer both need a bit of positive dihedral. This makes it somewhat tricky to fasten them to the fuselage. Begin by making sure the fuselage extends one inch past the wing's leading edge.

Align the fuselage with the fold in the wing's middle. This fold forms a little ridge, and the soda straw sits right on top of that ridge.

Use three strips of tape to attach the wing to the fuselage, as shown in Illus. 240. Press the tape onto the straw, then around the straw, and then onto the under-side of the wing. The wing should have enough dihedral angle so that its tips are one-half inch higher than the wing's middle. Ask someone to lend an extra hand or two to hold the wing as you handle the fuselage and tape.

Attach the tail section in the same way. Illus. 241 shows this step. One or two strips of tape will do the job nicely, especially if you're using masking tape. Give this section a bit of dihedral as well.

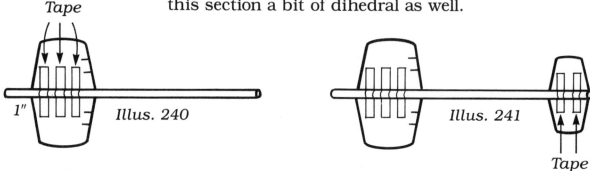

Illus. 240

Illus. 241

Dizzy is going to be catapult-launched, so construct a launching hook using a paper clip. Bend the paper clip open on one side so that it looks just like the one shown in Illus. 242.

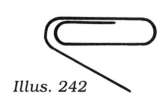

Illus. 242

To attach the launching hook to the airplane, slip one side of the clip inside the soda-straw fuselage, so that the hook looks like the one shown in Illus. 243.

Fasten the hook securely to the fuselage using a strip of tape wrapped firmly around both the nose of the fuselage and the hook. Illus. 243 shows the tape just starting to wrap around the hook.

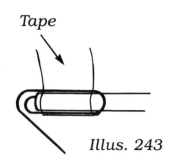

Illus. 243

Once the launching hook is attached, make your catapult, using a rubber band and a large paper clip. Slip the band into the clip and you'll have a catapult like the one shown in Illus. 244.

Another way to make a catapult is to roll a six-inch piece of paper into a tight roll. Bend the rolled paper in the middle and slip the rubber band into the fold. Secure the doubled roll of paper using several wraps of cellophane tape, so that it looks like the one shown in Illus. 245.

With your catapult made, it's time to test-launch *Dizzy*. You're probably better off flying *Dizzy* outdoors, but you can test it indoors if you're careful not to have anything breakable in the way.

Hook the launching hook over the rubber band and pull back on the airplane. Grasp *Dizzy* with your forefinger on top of the horizontal stabilizer; your thumb and your middle finger hold the rear of the fuselage. Illus. 246 shows how.

Pull back and let *Dizzy* go. It will tear out at real speed, so be careful where *Dizzy* is pointing when it is launched. Adjusting the wing flaps down makes *Dizzy* do a great loop. With one flap up higher than the other, *Dizzy* will bank and turn. Experiment by bending the stabilizer tips straight up to form little vertical stabilizers to give *Dizzy* a straighter flight.

Try launching *Dizzy* straight up, horizontally, and at various angles. Do this outdoors, please. Very few parents are pleased to have *Dizzy* crashing into the ceiling after a vertical launch!

Try some different wing and horizontal stabilizer shapes if you enjoy catapult-launched airplanes. The sky's the limit with experimental designs.

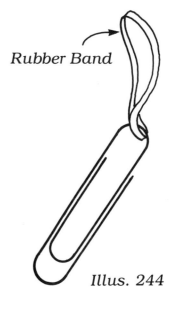

Rubber Band

Illus. 244

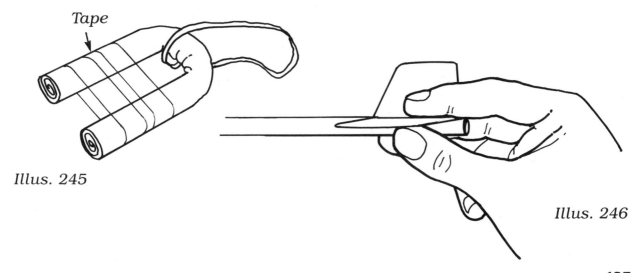

Tape

Illus. 245

Illus. 246

Metric Equivalents

INCHES TO MILLIMETRES AND CENTIMETRES

MM—millimetres　　*CM—centimetres*

Inches	MM	CM	Inches	CM	Inches	CM
⅛	3	0.3	9	22.9	30	76.2
¼	6	0.6	10	25.4	31	78.7
⅜	10	1.0	11	27.9	32	81.3
½	13	1.3	12	30.5	33	83.8
⅝	16	1.6	13	33.0	34	86.4
¾	19	1.9	14	35.6	35	88.9
⅞	22	2.2	15	38.1	36	91.4
1	25	2.5	16	40.6	37	94.0
1¼	32	3.2	17	43.2	38	96.5
1½	38	3.8	18	45.7	39	99.1
1¾	44	4.4	19	48.3	40	101.6
2	51	5.1	20	50.8	41	104.1
2½	64	6.4	21	53.3	42	106.7
2	76	7.6	22	55.9	43	109.2
3½	89	8.9	23	58.4	44	111.8
4	102	10.2	24	61.0	45	114.3
4½	114	11.4	25	63.5	46	116.8
5	127	12.7	26	66.0	47	119.4
6	152	15.2	27	68.6	48	121.9
7	178	17.8	28	71.1	49	124.5
8	203	20.3	29	73.7	50	127.0

INDEX